PASCAL

— a short self-instructional course

PASCAL
— a short self-instructional course

Michael Oatey
Principal Technical Author
International Computers Limited
and

Chris Clare
Principal Lecturer in Computing
Polytechnic of the South Bank, London

Pitman

PITMAN PUBLISHING LIMITED
128 Long Acre, London WC2E 9AN

PITMAN PUBLISHING INC
1020 Plain Street, Marshfield, Massachusetts 02050

Associated Companies
Pitman Publishing Pty Ltd, Melbourne
Pitman Publishing New Zealand Ltd, Wellington
Copp Clark Pitman, Toronto

© M J Oatey and C P Clare 1985

First published in Great Britain 1985

British Library Cataloguing in Publication Data

Oatey, Michael
　　Pascal: a short self-instructional course.
　　1. Pascal (Computer program language)
　　2. Microcomputers—Programming
　　I. Title　II. Clare, Chris
　　001.64′24　　QA76.73.P2

　　ISBN 0-273-02203-2

Photoset by Paston Press, Norwich
Printed in Great Britain at The Pitman Press, Bath

Contents

Acknowledgements

The authors would like to thank colleagues and students who have commented on or worked through drafts of this book, including in particular: Susy McPhee, Dilip Patel, Alan Pool, and Susan Stearman.

Introduction

Types of computer

Computers vary greatly in size and complexity. A very small computer can look rather like a typewriter keyboard attached to a television set; these are often called microcomputers. As you type on the keyboard, the characters appear on the screen. When you have typed in instructions and information, the computer will perform some operations and calculations and then print out the results on the screen.

At the other end of the scale, very large computer systems can consist of dozens or even hundreds of terminals (each looking like a microcomputer with a keyboard and video screen) linked to a central computer. Other equipment may also be added. For example, magnetic tape or disk may be used to store information; and a printer is often used to print out results on paper as an alternative to a video screen.

However, for immediate purposes we will assume the user (that is you) types in instructions on a keyboard and the results are displayed on a screen.

Computer languages

Instructions are given to a computer by means of codes or *languages*. One such language is Pascal, which is named after the seventeenth-century French philosopher and mathematician. The language was originally developed for teaching purposes, to encourage good programming methods. However, it is now also widely used by professionals and is becoming increasingly available on a wide range of computers.

A computer *program* consists of a series of instructions written in a computer language, such as Pascal. Programs can be written for tasks ranging from adding two numbers together to making airline seat reservations.

There are several versions of Pascal. In this book we refer to: Standard Pascal, which is the original version; UCSD Pascal, which is an enhanced version developed at the University of California at San Diego; and versions developed for small and home microcomputers.

Purpose of this book

As the title implies, the book does not provide a comprehensive coverage of Pascal. However, sufficient material is covered to allow you to write interesting and useful programs, and to provide a secure grounding if you wish to venture further into the language. Only non-mathematical applications are used, such as: calculating bills and test results; analyzing questionnaires; searching data; and sorting data into numerical or alphabetical order.

No previous experience of computers is assumed. However, you may find the course easier if you have had a little exposure to another computer language such as BASIC. (A companion volume on BASIC is available which, where appropriate, uses the same approach and examples as the present book. See the back cover for details.)

How to use this book

The book is divided into eight main Units. Questions are interspersed within the text of each Unit. These questions are preceded by the symbol ◐, for example the following question appears on page 30 in Unit 3:

◐   Qu 3.1   Write a program called EG4 that will print out the result of adding together three integer numbers typed in by the user. Use variables called D, E, and F.

Answers are given at the bottom of the next page but one, so the answer to the above question appears at the bottom of page 32.

Always write down your answers before checking them. If you get an incorrect answer, re-read the preceding text and try to see where you went wrong.

Further questions are given at the end of each Unit. Answers to these questions are at the back of the book.

From time to time a series of Exercises are included, which consolidate material in all previous Units. Answers to the Exercises are at the back of the book.

Access to a computer

Continual access to a computer is not necessary. But occasional access is desirable, especially if you have not run a program on a computer before. A brief introduction to running a Pascal program on a computer is given in the Appendix (which you should read through even if you do not have access to a computer).

Even if you have immediate access, it is suggested you work through at least part of a Unit and answer one or two questions before trying programs on a computer.

Unit 1 Some simple programs

Below is a simple but complete Pascal program, which could be typed in on a computer keyboard. The program adds two numbers together:

```
PROGRAM ADDITION (OUTPUT);
BEGIN
   WRITELN (22 + 4);
END.
```

The first line contains the program heading, which starts with the word PROGRAM. The word PROGRAM is followed by the name of the program, which is chosen by the person writing the program; we have decided to call this program ADDITION. The program name is followed by the word OUTPUT enclosed in brackets, which specifies the program is to produce some results or output. Notice the line ends with a semicolon.

The second line of the program contains the word BEGIN, which shows the main body of the program is to start.

The main body of a Pascal program consists of one or more *statements*, which give instructions to the computer. When an instruction given by a statement is carried out, the statement is said to be *executed*.

The above program contains only one statement, namely a WRITELN statement. WRITELN stands for "write a line". The above WRITELN statement instructs the computer to write a line containing the result of 22 plus 4. When this statement is executed, the number 26 will be written out (or printed out if you like) on the video screen.

The last line of the above program contains the word END followed by a full stop. This shows the end of the program has been reached.

The next program, which we have called ADD, contains three WRITELN statements. Notice the program heading and the statements are followed by semicolons, and the last line ends with a full stop:

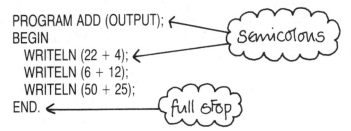

```
PROGRAM ADD (OUTPUT);
BEGIN
    WRITELN (22 + 4);
    WRITELN (6 + 12);
    WRITELN (50 + 25);
END.
```

Semicolons

full stop

When this program is executed or *run* on a computer, the following numbers will be printed out on the screen:

```
26
18
75
```

(*Note:* If you are not clear about what *running* a program means, you should refer to the Appendix, pages 111–112.)

The next program performs addition, subtraction, multiplication, and division. The * sign means multiplication and the / sign means division.

```
PROGRAM ARITHMETIC (OUTPUT);
BEGIN
    WRITELN (12 + 4);
    WRITELN (12 - 4);
    WRITELN (12 * 4);
    WRITELN (12 / 4);
END.
```

Note: If you run this program on a computer, you will find the result of the last WRITELN statement involving division is printed in a special form. The reason will be given later in this Unit.

Now answer the following question. (Remember answers appear at the bottom of the next page but one.)

◑ Qu 1.1   What is the name of the above program? What values will be printed out when this program is run?

There are four general points to be made on the programs given so far:

1 The program name is followed by the word OUTPUT enclosed in brackets. When a program is to produce output or results, some versions of Pascal, including Standard Pascal, require OUTPUT in the program heading; with other versions, including UCSD, OUTPUT in the program heading is optional; and with yet other versions, including some for small microcomputers, OUTPUT must be omitted. In this book we will include OUTPUT in the program heading as a reminder that it may sometimes be required.

2 Statements are indented. This is not essential but, as we shall see, indentation can make more complex programs easier to read.

3 Statements are followed by semicolons. Strictly, statements must be *separated* by semicolons, and a semicolon after the last statement is optional. However, use of semicolons is a common source of error in programs, and we feel it is a good habit to include semicolons even when they are optional.

4 Calculations in WRITELN statements are enclosed in brackets. Whatever is to be written out by a WRITELN statement must always be enclosed in brackets.

Try to bear these points in mind when answering the next question.

◑ Qu 1.2 Write a program called ARITH2 that will print out the results of the following: 18 minus 2, 24 divided by 6, and 13 multiplied by 7.

Combinations of symbols, such as 22 + 4 and 8 * 6 / 2, are called expressions. These expressions can include brackets, but cannot include currency signs. For example, the following statement finds the cost of four items at 20p each and nine items at 3p each:

```
WRITELN ((4 * 20) + (9 * 3));
```

Notice the outer brackets enclosing the whole expression are retained.

The brackets in the above expression are included only for clarification. But sometimes brackets are essential. In general, the usual rules for calculating arithmetic expressions are followed, including: multiplication and division before addition and subtraction, and all expressions in brackets calculated first. If you are not clear on these rules, you may need to refer to mathematics books or perhaps to more comprehensive books on Pascal (the problem is one of mathematics rather than computing). However, expressions in this book will be kept simple and, unless otherwise stated, brackets are used in expressions only for clarification and are not essential. But try to remember that expressions in brackets are always calculated first, for example:

$$(12 + 6) / 2 = 9$$
$$12 + (6 / 2) = 15$$

One final point on expressions. When multiplying, the * sign must always be included. So in the following expression, the * sign could not be omitted (and the brackets are also essential):

WRITELN (4 * (12 − 7));

❶ Qu 1.3   When the above WRITELN statement is executed, what will be printed out?

❶ Qu 1.4   Write a program called TEMPERATURE that will convert 60 degrees Fahrenheit to degrees Centigrade. (To convert Fahrenheit to Centigrade, *first* subtract 32 and then multiply by 5/9.)

Ans 1.1   The name of the program is ARITHMETIC. The following values will be printed out: 16, 8, 48, and 3.

The following statement will find the result of 25% of 160:

    WRITELN (160 * 0.25);

Notice the decimal number has been written as 0.25 with a leading zero. The leading zero must be included, so the following statement is incorrect:

    WRITELN (160 * .25);

leading zero omitted, causing an error

Qu 1.5   The price of an item is £20 plus tax at 15%. Write a program called TAX that first prints out the value of the tax, and then prints the total cost of the item including tax.

Print format

When the programs given so far in this Unit are run on a computer, the result of each WRITELN statement will be printed on a separate line of the screen. For example:

    PROGRAM ARITH3 (OUTPUT);
    BEGIN
       WRITELN (20 + 4);
       WRITELN (20 − 4);
       WRITELN (20 * 4);
    END.

will produce the following output when run:

    24
    16
    80

To print these results on one line of the screen, use one WRITELN statement and separate the expressions by commas:

Ans 1.2   PROGRAM ARITH2 (OUTPUT);
          BEGIN
             WRITELN (18 − 2);
             WRITELN (24 / 6);
             WRITELN (13 * 7);
          END.

```
PROGRAM ARITH4 (OUTPUT);
BEGIN
    WRITELN (20 + 4, 20 − 4, 20 * 4);
END.
```

which will produce the output:

24 16 80

The commas themselves are not printed.

    We have left one space between each number printed on the line. The actual number of spaces left varies between computers. It is also possible to include formatting information to specify any particular spacing. Formatting information is explained in the Appendix (page 114) but we give a brief example here. In the statement:

WRITELN (20 * 4 :3);   *formatting information*

the number 3 after the colon specifies the output is to take up 3 spaces. The actual result (80) takes up two spaces, so an extra space is left before the number to make up the three spaces.

    In this book we will not include formatting information in WRITELN statements, and will simply assume that numbers printed on a line are normally separated by one space. But if you have access to a computer, refer to the Appendix and try experimenting with formatting information.

◑   Qu 1.6   Write a program called PERCENTAGES that will print the following percentages on one line of the screen: 8% of 180, 15% of 40, and 8% of 4.2.

Ans 1.3   20

Ans 1.4   PROGRAM TEMPERATURE (OUTPUT);
           BEGIN
              WRITELN ((60 − 32) * 5/9);
           END.
The brackets enclosing 60 − 32 are essential.

Real numbers

The last topic in this Unit concerns decimal numbers, including how they are printed out.

In Pascal, numbers that have a decimal or fractional part are called *real* numbers (e.g. 4.2 and 16.33), while whole numbers that have no decimal or fractional part are called *integer* numbers (e.g. 4 and 16). It is as well to get used to these terms now because in later Units we will have to specify whether numbers in programs are real or integer.

So far in this Unit we have seen only examples of integer output, which is printed as we might expect. But real numbers can be printed in a different form. For example, when the following statement is executed:

WRITELN (12 + 6.9);

the result will be printed in a form like:

1.89E01

which means 1.89 with the decimal point moved one place to the right (that is 18.9). This E notation (or floating point notation to give it the full name) is useful for printing very large or very small numbers, but otherwise can be rather cumbersome.

It is possible to avoid the E notation by including further formatting information in WRITELN statements, which is described in the Appendix (page 115). As stated earlier we will not include formatting information in this book and, to avoid the E notation, we will simply assume all real numbers are printed in the normal form to one place of decimals. But if you run programs on a computer, you must expect output of real numbers in E notation unless you include formatting information.

Leaving aside output format, it is important to clearly distinguish between real and integer numbers for future purposes. Note in particular that 12.0 is a real number, even though the fractional part is zero. Also any expression that includes a real number will yield a real result, for example:

Ans 1.5   PROGRAM TAX (OUTPUT);
        BEGIN
          WRITELN (20 * 0.15);
          WRITELN ((20 * 0.15) + 20);
        END.

10 + 4.5   (result 15.5)
10 * 0.5   (result 5.0)
12.0 − 4   (result 8.0)

Lastly, the result of division using the / sign is *always* real. This is why after the program called ARITHMETIC on page 5 we said the result of the last WRITELN statement involving division would be printed in a special form. (When dividing one integer by another, it is possible to produce an integer result by substituting DIV for the / sign. However, we will not use DIV in this book and will not consider this option further.)

The following examples illustrate the rules on real and integer numbers we have looked at in this Unit:

Statement	Result
WRITELN (8 + 4);	integer
WRITELN (8 + 4.0);	real
WRITELN (8 * 4);	integer
WRITELN (8 * 4.0);	real
WRITELN (8 / 4);	real
WRITELN (8 / 4.0);	real
WRITELN (8 + .4);	(error)

The last statement above will produce an error because .4 should be written as 0.4 as we saw earlier. Similarly 12.0 cannot be written as 12. without the trailing zero. These examples provide a general rule that there must be at least one digit on either side of a decimal point in real numbers.

◐ Qu 1.7   State whether the following statements will produce a real or integer result, or an error:

(a) WRITELN (0.3 * 30);
(b) WRITELN (30 * 30);
(c) WRITELN (30 / 30);
(d) WRITELN (30 − .3);
(e) WRITELN (3.0 + 30);

Ans 1.6   PROGRAM PERCENTAGES (OUTPUT);
        BEGIN
          WRITELN (180 * 0.08, 40 * 0.15, 4.2 * 0.08);
        END.

Summary (Unit 1)

○ Pascal programs start with a program heading, which consists of the word PROGRAM, followed by the program name, followed by a semicolon. When a program is to produce some results or output, some versions of Pascal require the word OUTPUT enclosed in brackets after the program name; in other versions, OUTPUT is optional or must be omitted.

○ The main body of a Pascal program consists of one or more *statements*, which give instructions to the computer. Statements must be separated by semicolons.

○ The main body must be preceded by the word BEGIN and followed by the word END. The END must be followed by a full stop.

○ WRITELN statements can be used to print out the results of arithmetic expressions. The expressions must be enclosed in brackets. The following signs are used:

+ for addition
− for subtraction
* for multiplication
/ for division

Currency signs cannot be used in arithmetic expressions. Decimal numbers must have at least one digit on either side of the decimal point.

○ When two or more expressions, separated by commas, are included in a WRITELN statement, the output is printed across the screen. The spacing used varies between computers.

○ Numbers with a fractional part are called *real* numbers. Whole numbers without a fractional part are called *integer* numbers. Real numbers may be printed out using a special E notation.

○ Formatting information can be included in WRITELN statements to specify output spacing and specify how real numbers are to be printed (see Appendix, page 114).

Further questions

1.8   Identify any errors in the following program:

```
PROGRAM DEMO (OUTPUT);
BEGIN
   WRITELN (12 * 4, 6 * 3.2)
   WRITELN (12 / 4);
END
```

1.9   Write a program called COST that will print out the following results on separate lines of the screen:

Line 1: the total cost of 6 items at £5.95 each and 25 items at £0.49 each
Line 2: 8% of 5.95

1.10   Write a program called EXCHANGE that will print out the value of four pounds sterling in dollars. Assume a hypothetical exchange rate of 2.15 dollars to the pound.

1.11   The price of a desk is £55 plus tax at 10%. The price of a chair is £22 plus tax at 15%. Write a program called COST2 that will print out the following results on three lines of the screen:

Line 1: the cost of the desk including tax
Line 2: the cost of the chair including tax
Line 3: the tax on the desk followed by the tax on the chair

Answers to Further Questions are given at the end of the book

Ans 1.7   (a) real   (b) integer   (c) real   (d) error   (e) real

Unit 2 Assignment statements and variables; REPEAT statements and loops

Note: As well as complete programs, examples in this book will use parts of programs, called program *fragments*. Only complete programs can be run on a computer, and you should not attempt to run program fragments.

Below is a fragment from the program called ADDITION on page 4 (omitting the program heading for the moment):

```
BEGIN
  WRITELN (22 + 4);
END.
```

The following is an equivalent program fragment, which we will use to illustrate an assignment statement:

```
BEGIN
  A := 22 + 4;
  WRITELN (A);
END.
```

The assignment statement above instructs the computer to assign the result of 22 plus 4 to A. When this statement is executed, A will have the value of 26. (The WRITELN statement then prints out the value of A, that is 26). Notice the symbol for assignment is a colon followed by an equals sign (:=).

Below is another example of an assignment statement. Suppose E stands for the price of eggs, which are currently 7 pence each. This can be represented by the statement:

```
E := 7;
```

The following fragment can be used in a program to find the cost of six eggs:

```
BEGIN
  E := 7;
  WRITELN (E * 6);
END.
```

Now suppose the price of eggs goes up to 9 pence each. We can insert two more lines in the fragment:

```
BEGIN
  E := 7;
  WRITELN (E * 6);
  E := 9;
  WRITELN (E * 6);
END.
```

After the second assignment statement, the value of E is changed from 7 to 9. (You may be thinking that a shorter sequence could be written similar to programs in Unit 1. This is true of several examples in this Unit, but we are using this approach to illustrate some important ideas in a simple way.)

E will take different values during the running of a program containing the above fragment: after the first assignment statement E has the value 7, and after the second assignment statement E has the value 9 (the old value of 7 is lost). For this reason, symbols such as E or A (or B or C etc.) are called *variables* in Pascal. Their value can vary.

◑ Qu 2.1   Write an assignment statement that will give the value of 98.4 to the variable T.

Pascal allows more meaningful names for variables than just letters such as A or E. For example, the price of eggs can be called EGGS and we can write:

```
EGGS := 7;
```

Variable names are decided by the programmer and should be chosen to make a program as readable as possible. For example, if we use the following variable names in a program on test scores:

    MARKS1 for marks in the first test
    MARKS2 for marks in the second test
    MARKS3 for marks in the third test
    TOTAL   for total marks

then this statement can be readily followed:

    TOTAL := MARKS1 + MARKS2 + MARKS3;

General rules for variable names are:

* Only letters and digits can be used (hence hyphens, commas, spaces, etc. cannot be included).

* The first character must be a letter.

* Any number of characters can be used, but there is a limit on the number recognized by the computer. Here we assume a limit of six characters (the rest are ignored). So all names in the same program must differ in the first six characters by at least one character. (For example, NUMBER1 and NUMBER2 cannot be used in the same program, but NUM1 and NUM2 can be used.)

* Key words with other uses in the program, such as BEGIN, END, OUTPUT, and WRITELN, cannot be used. These are called *reserved* words.

The same rules apply to program names and to other names in Pascal. Collectively, these names are called *identifiers*.

◑ Qu 2.2   Which of the following variable names are illegal? (a) TEMPERATURE (b) NUM-OF-EGGS   (c) NUMEGGS   (d) NUM EGGS   (e) 6X   (f) A4B3   (g) END

◑ Qu 2.3   Write a statement that calculates distance travelled (use the variable DIST) given the initial mileage (use the variable STARTMILES) and the final mileage (use the variable ENDMILES).

So far in this Unit we have looked only at program fragments. Now we turn to complete programs that contain variables. In a complete program, any variables used must be *declared* in a variable declaration. This declaration comes between the program heading and the main body, and begins with the word VAR, for example:

```
PROGRAM GROCERIES (OUTPUT);
VAR        EGGS: REAL;
BEGIN
   EGGS := 8.5;
   WRITELN (EGGS * 6);
END.
```

data type

The variable declaration in this program consists of the word VAR, followed by a variable name (EGGS), followed by a colon and the word REAL, and ends with a semicolon. The word following the colon specifies the *type* of data the variable can take. Here we have specified type REAL, which means the variable EGGS can take decimal values (as explained in Unit 1). Other data types can be specified, including INTEGER.

In the next program, four variables are used all declared as type INTEGER, which means they can take only whole number values and not decimal values. Notice the variables are separated by commas in the VAR declaration:

```
PROGRAM TESTMARKS (OUTPUT);
VAR        MARKS1, MARKS2, MARKS3, TOTAL: INTEGER;
BEGIN
   MARKS1 := 65;
   MARKS2 := 35;
   MARKS3 := 20;
   TOTAL   := MARKS1 + MARKS2 + MARKS3;
   WRITELN (TOTAL / 3);
END.
```

The general format of the VAR declaration is:

VAR *variable-list: type;*

where *variable-list* can contain one variable, or two or more variables separated by commas; and *type* specifies the type of data the variables

---

Ans 2.1   T := 98.4;

in the list can take. More than one *variable-list* followed by *type* can be included in a VAR declaration (for example, see the program called HOTEL1 on page 48).

◑ Qu 2.4 Write a VAR declaration for a program that uses variables with the following names: TOTAL, TAX, and NET. Declare the variables as type REAL.

Variables can be used in expressions in WRITELN statements as described in Unit 1. Again, if there are two or more expressions in a WRITELN statement separated by commas, results are printed across the screen. For example:

```
PROGRAM DEMO (OUTPUT);
VAR        A, B: INTEGER;
BEGIN
  A := 6;
  B := 4;
  WRITELN (A, B, A + B, A – B, A * B);
END.
```

could produce the following output when run:

6 4 10 2 24

The next program calculates the interest charges on an amount borrowed:

```
PROGRAM INTEREST (OUTPUT);
VAR        AMOUNT, RATE: REAL;
BEGIN
  AMOUNT := 180.0;
  RATE := 0.1;
  WRITELN (AMOUNT, AMOUNT * RATE);
END.
```

Ans 2.2   The following are illegal: (b), (d), (e), (g)

Ans 2.3   DIST := ENDMILES – STARTMILES;

◑ Qu 2.5 When the above program called INTEREST is run, what will be printed out?

◑ Qu 2.6 A program that calculates electricity charges uses the following integer variables:

> OLD for the previous meter reading
> NEW for the present meter reading
> UNITS for the units supplied

Write a program called ELECTRICITY that gives OLD the value 62848 and NEW the value 63178, and then calculates UNITS. The program should then print out the following four items on one line of the screen: the values of NEW, OLD, UNITS, and the charge, given that the price per unit is 4.5 pence.

Store locations and variables

All computers have a store, or memory, where instructions and data needed to run a program are held. It can be helpful if you realize that variables, such as A and B, refer to physical locations in the computer's store:

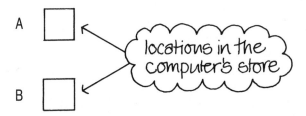

Now consider this sequence of statements:

```
A := 3;
WRITELN (A);
A := 8;
```

After the first assignment statement, the value stored in location A is 3:

A [3]

After the second assignment statement, the value stored in location A is changed to 8:

A

Of course the computer does not actually cross out the 3. Rather the 3 is deleted completely and replaced by the 8. In more technical language, the 3 is overwritten by the 8. But for our purposes it is convenient to represent the overwriting by crossing out the old value.

Below is another sequence, together with the values stored in locations A and B after each statement is executed:

	A	B
A := 5;	5	?
WRITELN (A);	5	?
B := A + 2;	5	7

Notice after the first assignment statement we do not know what value is stored in location B. But whatever this value is, it will be overwritten when the second assignment statement is executed.

In the next sequence, the last statement may look rather odd at first:

```
A := 1;
WRITELN (A);
A := A + 7;
```

However, if you consider it in terms of values stored in locations, it makes sense:

Ans 2.4   VAR TOTAL, TAX, NET: REAL;

A

A := 1;   [1]

WRITELN (A);   [1]

A := A + 7;   [~~1~~ 8]

The last statement is instructing the computer to add 7 to the value already in location A and then store the result in location A.

Qu 2.7   When the following program fragment is executed, what will be printed out?
```
B := 10;
B := B - 4;
WRITELN (B);
```

Qu 2.8   When the following program fragment is executed, what will be printed out?
```
A := 1;
N := 26;
A := A + N;
WRITELN (A);
WRITELN (N);
```

Ans 2.5   180.0 18.0

Ans 2.6   PROGRAM ELECTRICITY (OUTPUT);
```
VAR      OLD, NEW, UNITS: INTEGER;
BEGIN
  OLD := 62848;
  NEW := 63178;
  UNITS := NEW - OLD;
  WRITELN (NEW, OLD, UNITS, UNITS * 4.5);
END.
```

REPEAT statements and loops

Now consider the following program:

```
PROGRAM NUM1 (OUTPUT);
VAR      N: INTEGER;
BEGIN
  N := 1;
  WRITELN (N);
  N := N + 2;
  WRITELN (N);
  N := N + 2;
  WRITELN (N);
  N := N + 2;
  WRITELN (N);
END.
```

◗   Qu 2.9   When the above program called NUM1 is run, what will be printed out?

This program is already repetitious and prints out only four numbers. Suppose we wanted to print all odd numbers between 1 and 99 or between 1 and 9999. Such a program would be extremely long and tedious.
   An alternative way of writing the NUM1 program above is:

```
PROGRAM NUM2 (OUTPUT);
VAR      N: INTEGER;
BEGIN
  N := 1;
  REPEAT
    WRITELN (N);
    N := N + 2;
  UNTIL N > 7;
END.
```

program loops back until N is greater than 7

The statements between REPEAT and UNTIL are repeatedly executed until N reaches a value greater than 7 (the > symbol means "greater than"). So the program loops between the REPEAT and UNTIL lines until N is greater than 7, when the program drops through to the final END.

Note carefully that although N has the value of 9 at the end of the last loop, the number 9 is not printed out:

```
REPEAT
    WRITELN (N);
    N := N + 2;  ←
UNTIL N > 7;
```

N equals 9 on the last loop

The next program uses a similar REPEAT loop:

```
PROGRAM NUM3 (OUTPUT);
VAR      N: INTEGER;
BEGIN
  N := 5;
  REPEAT
    WRITELN (N);
    N := N + 5;
  UNTIL N > 100;
END.
```

◑ Qu 2.10   When the above program NUM3 is run, what series of numbers will be printed out?

◑ Qu 2.11   Write a program NUM4 that will print out every even number between 2 and 1000 inclusive. Use an integer variable called N.

Although we are using loops here for the rather trivial task of printing out simple number series, the principle of looping is extremely important in computer programming. We shall see further applications of loops in the next Unit.

Ans 2.7   6

Ans 2.8   27
          26

General formats and layout

From now on in this book we will give general formats of all declarations and statements, which can be very useful for reference and as memory joggers. We have already seen the general format of the VAR declaration (page 17):

> VAR *variable-list*: *type*;

The general format of the REPEAT statement is:

> REPEAT
>   *statement-sequence*;
> UNTIL *condition*;

where *statement-sequence* can contain one statement, or two or more statements separated by semicolons. Examples of a *condition* we have used in this Unit are N > 7 and N > 100. Other forms of condition will be given later.

We will follow the general format of all statements by a semicolon. The semicolon is not part of the statement, but serves as a reminder that a semicolon must be added if another statement follows.

Pascal allows complete freedom in laying out declarations and statements. For example, a VAR declaration could be laid out as:

> VAR
>   *variable-list*:
>   *type*;

The general format gives the components of a declaration or statement in the order they must occur, but the layout can be freely varied.

Ans 2.9   1
           3
           5
           7

Summary (Unit 2)

○ *Variables* are used to represent different numbers or quantities in a program. Variables are so called because their value can vary during the running of a program.

○ Rules for variable names are given on page 16. The same rules apply to program names.

○ Variables must be declared in a VAR declaration, which comes between the program heading and the main body. A general format is:

VAR *variable-list*: *type*;

where *variable-list* contains one or more variables separated by commas, and *type* specifies the type of data the variables in the list can hold. More than one *variable-list* followed by *type* can be included in a VAR declaration.

○ Assignment statements assign values to variables. The symbol for assignment is a colon followed by an equals sign (:=).

○ The value of a variable is held in a location in the computer's store. A useful way of thinking about a statement such as:

N := N + 1

is that it adds 1 to the value already in location N and then stores the result in location N.

○ The general format of the REPEAT statement is:

REPEAT
  statement-sequence;
UNTIL *condition*;

where *statement-sequence* contains one or more statements separated by semicolons. The *statement-sequence* is executed repeatedly until the *condition* is satisfied.

Ans 2.10 and 2.11   See page 26

Further questions

2.12 The tax on the first £200 of pay is zero. All pay above £200 is taxed at 35%. Assuming pay (PAY) does exceed £200, write a fragment of three statements that first calculates taxable pay (TAXABLE), then calculates tax (TAX), and then prints out the pay and tax on one line of the screen.

2.13 When the following program is run, what will be printed out?

```
PROGRAM DEMO (OUTPUT);
VAR        A, B: INTEGER;
BEGIN
  A := 4;
  B := 10;
  B := B * A;
  WRITELN (B, A);
END.
```

2.14 A program uses the following real variables:

```
PRICE    = price of a meal
VAT      = value added tax
SERVICE = service charge
TOTAL    = total charge
```

Write a program that gives PRICE the value of 7.5 and then calculates VAT (which is 15% of the meal price) and SERVICE (which is 10% of the meal price). After calculating the total charge, the program should print out the values of PRICE, VAT, SERVICE, and TOTAL on one line of the screen. Call the program MEAL.

2.15 When the following program is run, what will be printed out?

```
PROGRAM DEMO (OUTPUT);
VAR        N: INTEGER;
BEGIN
  N := 0;
  REPEAT
    WRITELN (N);
    N := N + 1;
  UNTIL N > 250;
END.
```

Ans 2.10 Every fifth number between 5 and 100 inclusive.

Ans 2.11
```
PROGRAM NUM4 (OUTPUT);
VAR        N: INTEGER;
BEGIN
  N := 2;
  REPEAT
    WRITELN (N);
    N := N + 2;
  UNTIL N > 1000;
END.
```

Unit 3 READ statements and input data

The programs given so far have produced *output* or results but have not required any *input* of data while the program is running on the computer. This Unit considers how the user can input data, by typing on the keyboard, while the program is running.

When a program is to receive input, some versions of Pascal, including Standard, require the word INPUT in the program heading, for example:

```
PROGRAM EXAMPLE (INPUT, OUTPUT);
```

The word INPUT comes before OUTPUT, and the words are separated by a comma. With other versions of Pascal, including UCSD, the word INPUT (like OUTPUT) is optional in the program heading. And with yet other versions, including some for small microcomputers, both words must be omitted.

READ statements allow the user to input data while the program is running. Here is an example:

```
PROGRAM EXAMPLE1 (INPUT, OUTPUT);
VAR        A: INTEGER;
BEGIN
    READ (A); ←——————————————— READ statement
    WRITELN (A * 2);
END.
```

When the READ statement is reached, the program expects the user to type in some data. The program waits until the data is typed and the RETURN key is pressed. (In this book, we assume the RETURN key must be pressed to make data available to a program. The RETURN key also causes a carriage return. For further details, see the Appendix, pages 113 and 114).

Suppose the program is running and the user now types 12 and presses RETURN. The READ statement assigns the value of 12 to A. Then the WRITELN statement is executed and the number 24 is printed on the screen:

12
24

(The position on the screen of the input and output data can vary between versions of Pascal.)

The following program could give the same result as the program EXAMPLE1 above:

```
PROGRAM EG2 (OUTPUT);
VAR       A: INTEGER;
BEGIN
  A := 12;
  WRITELN (A * 2);
END.
```

The difference is that with the assignment statement, the value 12 is fixed before the program is run. With the READ statement, the value 12 is given when the program is actually running on the computer.

More than one variable can be included in a READ statement, provided the variables are separated by commas. The next program contains a READ statement that includes two variables, and the user is now expected to type in two data values:

```
PROGRAM EG3 (INPUT, OUTPUT);
VAR       A, B: INTEGER;
BEGIN
  READ (A, B);
  WRITELN (A * B);
END.
```

When typing in a real or integer value, the user must follow the value by at least one space or by pressing RETURN (so the computer can recognize the end of the value). Suppose the program EG3 above is running, and the user types 6, a space, 11, and then presses RETURN. The variable A is assigned the value 6 and the variable B the value 11. So the program prints out 66:

6 11
66

The general format of the READ statement is:

    READ (*variable-list*);

where *variable-list* contains one or more variables separated by commas.

◐ Qu 3.1   Write a program called EG4 that will print out the result of adding together three integer numbers typed in by the user. Use variables called D, E, and F.

The user should type in as many data values as there are variables in the READ statement. So this statement:

    READ (A, B, C, D, E, F);

requires the user to type in six values. If too few are typed, the program will wait indefinitely for the missing values. If too many are typed, the extra values may be read by a subsequent READ statement in the program.

Now let us look at a more practical application, such as programs for currency conversion that might be used by a bank or an exchange bureau. Below are the kind of statements we might expect to see in a program that converts dollars to francs, using a hypothetical exchange rate of 5 francs to the dollar:

    READ (DOLLARS);
    WRITELN (DOLLARS * 5);

It would be very useful to be able to repeatedly execute such statements for different values of DOLLARS. One possibility is to use the REPEAT statement we saw in Unit 2. The approach is shown below, omitting for the moment the condition following UNTIL:

    REPEAT
      READ (DOLLARS);
       WRITELN (DOLLARS * 5);
      UNTIL . . . ;

Now how do we break out of the loop when there is no more input data? We could arrange for the user (for example a bank clerk) to type a special number when he has finished, say −99. Now the REPEAT statement becomes:

```
REPEAT
    READ (DOLLARS);
    WRITELN (DOLLARS * 5);
    UNTIL DOLLARS = -99;
```

end of data marker

Here the −99 is acting as an "end of data marker" showing there is no more input data. Any number can be chosen as an end of data marker provided that it is impossible or extremely unlikely that the number will occur in the input data.

Unfortunately there is a problem with this approach. Answering the next question may help you to see it.

◖ **Qu 3.2** What, if anything, is printed out when the user types −99?

The −99 value is treated as input data so before breaking out of the loop the program prints out a meaningless negative number. This is not very satisfactory, and worse can happen when end of data markers are treated as input data as we shall see later.

We can avoid these problems by placing a READ statement immediately before the UNTIL so that the program breaks out of the loop *immediately* −99 is typed in. Now an extra READ statement is needed outside the loop to read the first data value:

```
READ (DOLLARS);
REPEAT
    WRITELN (DOLLARS * 5);
    READ (DOLLARS);
    UNTIL DOLLARS = -99;
```

input values can be immediately tested for end of data

This is a great improvement—but there is still a drawback!

◖ **Qu 3.3** Can you see what the drawback is?

If there is no input data (no customers!) then typing −99 once will not break out of the loop. The user must type −99 twice, and even then a meaningless negative number will be printed out. For the present we will assume there is always some input data, while noting this approach does not satisfactorily cater for cases where there is no input data.

◑ **Qu 3.4** Write a program called EXCHANGE that converts pounds to dollars, using a hypothetical exchange rate of 2.15 dollars to the pound. The user should be able to type in repeatedly a number of pounds to be converted and then type −99 when he has finished. Use a real variable called POUNDS. (Assume there will always be some input data.)

The currency conversion program can be modified to allow the user to type in the exchange rate at the time the program is run. In the following program, notice the exchange rate (DOLLARATE) need be typed in once only (say at the beginning of a day or a session):

```
PROGRAM EXCH2 (INPUT, OUTPUT);
VAR       POUNDS, DOLLARATE: REAL;
BEGIN
   READ (DOLLARATE);  ←——————  rate need be
   READ (POUNDS);                typed once only
   REPEAT
     WRITELN (POUNDS * DOLLARATE);
     READ (POUNDS);
   UNTIL POUNDS = −99;
END.
```

The two READ statements could be combined into one:

```
READ (DOLLARATE, POUNDS);
```

However, using two statements is perhaps clearer in this case.

Ans 3.1
```
PROGRAM EG4 (INPUT, OUTPUT);
VAR       D, E, F: INTEGER;
BEGIN
   READ (D, E, F);
   WRITELN (D + E + F);
END.
```

Qu 3.5 Write a program called TAX that will print out the sales tax on an item when the cost is typed in. Make it possible to type in the cost of items repeatedly, but the tax rate need be typed once only. Use −99 as the end of data marker, and use real variables called COST and TAXRATE. (Assume there will always be some input data.)

Totals

Programs that repeatedly read in and process data very often calculate running totals of quantities. For example, the currency conversion programs may keep running totals of money taken in and paid out (which could be used to check cash balances at the end of the day).

The general approach to keeping totals is shown by the following fragment, which keeps a running total of dollars taken in:

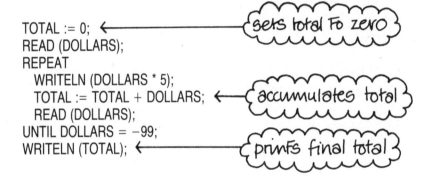

```
TOTAL := 0;              sets total to zero
READ (DOLLARS);
REPEAT
   WRITELN (DOLLARS * 5);
   TOTAL := TOTAL + DOLLARS;    accumulates total
   READ (DOLLARS);
UNTIL DOLLARS = −99;
WRITELN (TOTAL);         prints final total
```

Notice that TOTAL is set to zero initially. The reason is that before the statement:

TOTAL := TOTAL + DOLLARS;

is executed, TOTAL must be assigned a value (which in this case needs to be zero). Suppose the first number of dollars typed in by the user is 14. Then on the first execution of the above statement, the value of TOTAL is given by:

TOTAL := 0 + 14;

Ans 3.2   −495

Ans 3.3   The answer is given in the text following the question. If you want a hint, consider what happens if there is no input data.

If TOTAL does not have an initial value, the statement would be in effect:

TOTAL := ? + 14

which is meaningless and would cause an error in the program.

Note: With some computers, real and integer variables are set to zero automatically at the start of a program. However, other computers do not perform this function and in this book we will assume such variables are not set to zero automatically.

The REPEAT loop in the program fragment above could be written as follows (reversing the first two statements) with exactly the same result:

```
REPEAT
  TOTAL := TOTAL + DOLLARS;
  WRITELN (DOLLARS * 5);
  READ (DOLLARS);
UNTIL DOLLARS = -99;
```

But the READ statement *must* still come immediately before the UNTIL, so that values read can be immediately tested for end of data. If the TOTAL assignment statement came after the READ statement, the −99 end of data marker would be treated as input data and included in the total, giving the wrong result. Think about it!

◖ Qu 3.6 Rewrite the program in Qu 3.5 so that when the user types in −99, the program also prints out the total cost of all items (TOTCOST).

Ans 3.4
```
PROGRAM EXCHANGE (INPUT, OUTPUT);
VAR       POUNDS: REAL;
BEGIN
  READ (POUNDS);
  REPEAT
    WRITELN (POUNDS * 2.15);
    READ (POUNDS);
  UNTIL POUNDS = -99;
END.
```

Real and integer variables

To finish this Unit, we will return to the topic of real and integer variables. The reason for the distinction is that accounting for the decimal point in real values is quite a complicated operation for the computer, and hence integer values can be handled more easily than real values. If we can specify that a variable is to hold only integer values, efficiency is increased since there is no need to arrange for decimal points.

An integer variable cannot be given a real value (because the variable cannot deal with the decimal point). But a real variable can be given an integer value (in fact, the integer value is converted to a real value, so 9 would be held as the equivalent of 9.0). Therefore, if a variable is to hold real values or a mixture of real and integer values, it must be declared as type REAL. But if a variable is to hold only integer values, it should be declared as type INTEGER.

An example occurs in the program called HOTEL1 on page 48, which calculates hotel charges based on nights stayed. The variable NIGHTS is integer (this hotel does not provide fractions of a night), but the variables RATE and CHARGE are real since they may hold decimal numbers (in pounds and pence, such as 12.5).

From now on in questions, you must decide between REAL and INTEGER types for variables unless guidance is given.

◑   Qu 3.7   State whether real or integer variables should be used to hold values for: (a) airline seats, (b) bank balances, (c) votes, (d) bottles of wine, (e) distances (in kilometers and meters).

Ans 3.5
```
PROGRAM TAX (INPUT, OUTPUT);
VAR      COST, TAXRATE: REAL;
BEGIN
  READ (TAXRATE);
  READ (COST);
  REPEAT
    WRITELN (COST * TAXRATE);
    READ (COST);
  UNTIL COST = -99;
END.
```

Summary (Unit 3)

○ READ statements allow the user to type in data values at the time the program is run on the computer. A real or integer value must be followed by at least one space or by pressing RETURN.

○ The general format of the READ statement is:

READ (*variable-list*);

where *variable-list* contains one or more variables separated by commas. Values typed in by the user are assigned to the variables in the *variable-list*.

○ When a program is to receive input data, some versions of Pascal require the word INPUT in the program heading; in other versions, INPUT is optional or must be omitted.

○ End of data markers identify the end of a series of input data values. Care must be taken to avoid treating an end of data marker as input data. When using end of data markers, the REPEAT statement cannot satisfactorily cater for the case where there is no input data.

○ Totals can be found by using statements such as:

TOTAL := TOTAL + N;

TOTAL must be set to zero initially.

○ Real variables can be given real or integer values. Integer variables can be given only integer values. It is more efficient to use an integer variable when only integer values are to be held.

Ans 3.6   See page 37

Further questions

3.7 Refer to Qu 2.14 on page 26. Modify the program to allow the user to type in the price of the meal at the time the program is run.

3.8 Write a program called WEIGHT that will convert kilograms (KILOS) to pounds, given one kilogram equals 2.2 pounds. The user should be able to repeatedly type in a number of kilograms to be converted and then type −1 when he has finished. (Assume there will always be some input data.)

3.9 Write a program called TIME that converts hours (HRS) and minutes (MINS) into minutes. Assume the user will type in the hours and the minutes on the same line on the screen.

3.10 A gas bill consists of a standing charge (STANDING) plus a rate per unit consumed (RATE). Write a program called GASBILL that will print out the total charge (CHARGE) when the number of units consumed (UNITS) is typed in. The user should be able to type in a number of gas units repeatedly, but the standing charge and the rate need to be typed in once only. When the user types in −99, the program should print out the total of all charges (TOTAL) and then end. (Assume there will always be some input data.)

Ans 3.6 PROGRAM TAX (INPUT, OUTPUT);
     VAR   COST, TAXRATE, TOTCOST: REAL;
     BEGIN
       TOTCOST := 0;
       READ (TAXRATE);
       READ (COST);
       REPEAT
         WRITELN (COST * TAXRATE);
         TOTCOST := TOTCOST + COST;
         READ (COST);
       UNTIL COST = −99;
       WRITELN (TOTCOST);
     END.

Ans 3.7 (a) integer   (b) real   (c) integer   (d) integer   (e) real

Unit 4 WHILE statements and loops; IF statements and decisions

Before considering WHILE and IF statements, we need to introduce the concept of a *compound statement*. A compound statement consists of two or more single statements enclosed between BEGIN and END brackets. For example, the following is a compound statement containing three single statements:

```
BEGIN
  TOTAL := TOTAL + N;
  WRITELN (TOTAL);
  READ (N);
END;
```

As always, the single statements within the compound statement must be separated by semicolons.

The reason for introducing the compound statement is that sometimes a sequence of single statements must be grouped between BEGIN and END brackets, which allows the sequence to be treated as one single statement.

WHILE statements

When setting up loops to read in data, we have seen the REPEAT statement is unsatisfactory in cases where there is no data to input. When there is a possibility of no input data, the WHILE statement should be used instead. The general format of the WHILE statement is:

```
WHILE condition DO
  statement;
```

where *statement* can be single or compound. The *statement* is executed repeatedly while the *condition* remains true.

Below is a program fragment containing a WHILE statement. The <> sign in the condition means "not equal to":

```
READ (DOLLARS);
WHILE DOLLARS <> -99 DO        end of data marker
   BEGIN
      WRITELN (DOLLARS * 5);
      READ (DOLLARS);
   END;
```

While DOLLARS does not have the value −99 (the end of data marker), the statements in the loop are executed repeatedly. Immediately DOLLARS equals −99, the program drops through to the line following END without executing the statements in the loop. Thus if the first value of DOLLARS is −99, the statements in the loop are not executed at all.

The following program will print out a final total of a series of integer numbers typed in by the user:

```
PROGRAM TOTAL (INPUT, OUTPUT);
VAR       NUMBER, SUM: INTEGER;
BEGIN
   SUM := 0;
   READ (NUMBER);
   WHILE NUMBER <> -99 DO
      BEGIN
         SUM := SUM + NUMBER;
         READ (NUMBER);
      END;
   WRITELN (SUM);
END.
```

Now if the first value typed in is −99, the WHILE loop is not entered and the program drops through to the WRITELN (SUM) statement.

◐   Qu 4.1   Suppose the above program called TOTAL is running on a computer, but there is no input data and the user types −99. What, if anything, will be printed out?

◐   Qu 4.2   Rewrite the program in Qu 3.4 on page 32 without assuming there will always be some input data.

The essential point is that with a WHILE loop, the condition is tested *before* entering the loop and hence the statements in the loop may never be executed. With a REPEAT loop, the condition is tested *after* entering the loop and hence the statements in the loop are always executed at least once.

When setting up a loop to read a data stream that terminates with an end of data marker, the WHILE statement is preferred because it can deal with the no input data case. So in future in this book, we will always use the WHILE statement with end of data markers. We introduced REPEAT statements before WHILE statements because, for the beginner, the REPEAT statement is perhaps easier to understand.

◑   Qu 4.3   Rewrite the program in Qu 3.5 on page 33 without assuming there will always be some input data.

IF statements

IF statements are used for making decisions in programs. Here is an example:

    IF CODE = 1 THEN TAXRATE := 0.3;

which means if CODE has the value of 1, then assign the value of 0.3 to
TAXRATE. One general format of the IF statement is:

    IF *condition* THEN *statement*;

In our example, the *condition* is "CODE has the value of 1" and the *statement*
is the assignment statement giving TAXRATE the value of 0.3. If the condition
is true, the statement following THEN is executed. If not, the statement
following THEN is ignored. In this way decisions can be made—which in this
case is whether or not CODE has the value of 1.
    Six forms of condition can be specified in IF statements:

    =   equal to
    >   greater than
    <   less than
    >=   greater than or equal to
    <=   less than or equal to
    <>   not equal to

The same condition forms can also be used in REPEAT and WHILE
statements.

Ans 4.1   0

Ans 4.2   PROGRAM EXCHANGE (INPUT, OUTPUT);
          VAR   POUNDS: REAL;
          BEGIN
            READ (POUNDS);
            WHILE POUNDS <> −99 DO
              BEGIN
                WRITELN (POUNDS * 2.15);
                READ (POUNDS);
              END;
          END.

Below is another example of an IF statement:

    IF AGE < 21 THEN WRITELN (AGE);

which can be used to instruct the computer to print out a person's age if that person is under 21.

◐ Qu 4.4 Write a statement that will assign the value of 2.5 to COST if WEIGHT is less than or equal to 30.

◐ Qu 4.5 Write a statement that will print out a number provided that number is over 100. Use a variable called NUMBER.

Another format of the IF statement is:

    IF *condition* **THEN** *statement-1* **ELSE** *statement-2*;

If the *condition* is true, then *statement-1* is executed. Otherwise *statement-2* is executed. For example:

    IF PRICE > 25000 THEN DUTY := 0.02 ELSE DUTY := 0.01;

Here if price (say of a house) is over £25,000, the duty payable is 2%. If price is £25,000 or less, the duty is 1%.
    To make programs more readable, the IF-ELSE statement is often written in the form:

    IF *condition*
    THEN *statement-1*
    ELSE *statement-2*;

```
Ans 4.3   PROGRAM TAX (INPUT, OUTPUT);
          VAR     COST, TAXRATE: REAL;
          BEGIN
            READ (TAXRATE);
            READ (COST);
            WHILE COST <> -99 DO
              BEGIN
                WRITELN (COST * TAXRATE);
                READ (COST);
              END;
          END.
```

with the THEN and ELSE aligned under the IF. Notice that however the statement is written, there must be no semicolon before ELSE.

Here is a complete program using an IF-ELSE statement:

```
PROGRAM PAYTAX (INPUT, OUTPUT);
VAR        PAY, TAXRATE: REAL;
BEGIN
   READ (PAY);
   IF PAY > 5000
   THEN TAXRATE := 0.35
   ELSE TAXRATE := 0.25;
   WRITELN (PAY, TAXRATE);
END.
```

no semicolon before ELSE

● Qu 4.6 Suppose the above program TAXRATE is running on a computer. What will be printed out if the user types in (a) 7500, and (b) 5000?

● Qu 4.7 When SALES are below £1000, then BONUS is £15. In other cases BONUS is £45. Write a program called PERK that will print out the value of sales followed by the value of the bonus on the same line of the screen. The user should be able to type in the value of sales at the time the program is run. Use integer variables.

A final point on the IF statement general format is that *statement-1* and *statement-2* can be compound. Below is an example, which is taken from a payroll program where all hours worked over 40 are paid at an overtime rate:

```
IF HRS <= 40
THEN PAY := HRS * RATE
ELSE BEGIN
        OVERTIME := HRS − 40;
        PAY := (OVERTIME * OVERATE) + (40 * RATE);
     END;
```

It is possible for *statement-1* and *statement-2* in the general format to itself be an IF statement. This second IF statement is then said to be *nested*. The next example includes a nested IF statement:

```
IF CODE = 1
THEN WRITELN (RATE1)
ELSE IF CODE = 2
      THEN WRITELN (RATE2)
      ELSE WRITELN (RATE0);
```

} ← nested IF statement

Here if CODE equals 1 or 2, the program prints out the value of RATE1 or RATE2 respectively. If CODE has any other value, the program prints out the value of RATE0. Again, note there is no semicolon before an ELSE.

Further nesting can occur and great care must be taken on layout. In this book we will adopt the layout given above for nested IF statements (that is, aligning THEN and ELSE with the associated IF). Other layouts are commonly used—some better than others—and you may like to try experimenting when you become more proficient.

The next program provides a simple guessing game, in which the "player" is asked to type a number (say between 1 and 50). The player "wins" if he types a lucky number. In this program the lucky numbers are 17, 45, and 47. The player can have as many tries as he likes, and then type −9999 when he is fed up (which is likely to be pretty soon with this game!). Note that the statement WRITELN (0) will print out zero.

```
PROGRAM GAME1 (INPUT, OUTPUT);
VAR      N: INTEGER;
BEGIN
  READ (N);
  WHILE N <> −9999 DO
    BEGIN
      IF N = 17
      THEN WRITELN (N)
      ELSE IF N = 45
            THEN WRITELN (N)
            ELSE IF N = 47
                  THEN WRITELN (N)
                  ELSE WRITELN (0);
      READ (N);
    END;
END.
```

Ans 4.4   IF WEIGHT <= 30 THEN COST := 2.5;

Ans 4.5   IF NUMBER > 100 THEN WRITELN (NUMBER);

◑ Qu 4.8   Suppose the above program GAME1 is running on a computer. What number will be printed out if a player types in (a) 44, (b) 45, and (c) 46?

◑ Qu 4.9   Write a program called GAME2 for a similar guessing game with the following lucky numbers: 13, any number below 10, and any number above 45. If the player hits a lucky number, that number should be printed out. Otherwise zero should be printed out. The player should be able to type −9999 when he has finished.

Sometimes nested IF statements can be avoided. One possible alternative technique is to use multiple conditions in an IF statement. For example, the IF statement in GAME1 above can be written as:

```
IF (N = 17) OR (N = 45) OR (N = 47)
THEN WRITELN (N)
ELSE WRITELN (0);
```


Another option is the CASE statement, which is particularly useful when there are several conditions each with a different consequence.

Multiple conditions and CASE statements are not considered further in this book but if you continue studying Pascal, you should investigate these options (and find out which are available on your computer).

Ans 4.6   (a) 7500 0.35
              (b) 5000 0.25

Ans 4.7   PROGRAM PERK (INPUT, OUTPUT);
              VAR   SALES, BONUS: INTEGER;
              BEGIN
                READ (SALES);
                IF SALES < 1000
                THEN BONUS := 15
                ELSE BONUS := 45;
                WRITELN (SALES, BONUS);
              END.
Check you have no semicolon before ELSE.

Summary (Unit 4)

○ A *compound statement* is a sequence of two or more single statements enclosed between BEGIN and END brackets. The single statements must be separated by semicolons.

○ The WHILE statement general format is:

WHILE *condition* DO
　statement;

where *statement* can be single or compound. The *statement* is executed repeatedly while the *condition* remains true.

○ The IF statement is used for making decisions. The general format is:

IF *condition*
THEN *statement-1*
ELSE *statement-2*;

where *statement-1* and *statement-2* can be single or compound. If the *condition* is true, then *statement-1* is executed. Otherwise *statement-2* is executed. ELSE and *statement-2* can be omitted. There must be no semicolon before an ELSE. The layout is often varied.

○ The following condition forms can be used in IF, REPEAT, and WHILE statements:

```
=   equal to
>   greater than
<   less than
>=  greater than or equal to
<=  less than or equal to
<>  not equal to
```

Further questions

4.10 Write a program called EXAM that will allow the user to type in the marks gained by a candidate in three tests (use variables MARKS1, MARKS2, and MARKS3). The program should then add the marks together to obtain the total marks (TOTMARKS). The passmark is 45. The program should print out the total only if it equals or exceeds the passmark.

4.11 Write a program called HIGHER that will print out the higher of two unequal integer numbers typed in by the user. Use variables C and D.

4.12 Rewrite the program in Qu 3.10 on page 37 without assuming there will always be some input data.

Note: Exercises A, which follow, give further practice in the use of IF statements.

Ans 4.8   (a) 0   (b) 45   (c) 0

Ans 4.9   PROGRAM GAME2 (INPUT, OUTPUT);
        VAR   N: INTEGER;
        BEGIN
          READ (N);
          WHILE N <> −9999 DO
            BEGIN
              IF N = 13
              THEN WRITELN (N)
              ELSE IF N < 10
                    THEN WRITELN (N)
                    ELSE IF N > 45
                        THEN WRITELN (N)
                        ELSE WRITELN (0);
            READ (N);
          END;
        END.

Exercises A

These exercises are designed to consolidate the material in Units 1 to 4.

Exercise A-1

The following program will calculate hotel costs, given the number of NIGHTS stayed and the RATE per night. For two nights or less the rate is £12.5 per night. For up to six nights the rate is £10. For more than six nights the rate is £8 per night.

```
PROGRAM HOTEL1 (INPUT, OUTPUT);
VAR      NIGHTS: INTEGER;
              RATE, CHARGE: REAL;
BEGIN
   READ (NIGHTS);
   WHILE NIGHTS <> -99 DO
      BEGIN
         IF NIGHTS <= 2
         THEN RATE := 12.5
         ELSE IF NIGHTS <= 6
                 THEN RATE : = 10
                 ELSE RATE := 8;
         CHARGE := NIGHTS * RATE;
         WRITELN (NIGHTS, RATE, CHARGE);
         READ (NIGHTS);
      END;
   END.
```

Suppose this program is running on a computer. What values will be printed out if the user types (a) 11, (b) 6, and (c) −99?

Answers to Exercises are at the end of the book.

Exercise A-2

A hotel has the following charges:

1 night	£15
up to 7 nights	£12
up to 28 nights	£10
over 28 nights	£7.5

Write a program called HOTEL2 that will calculate charges, using the same variables and approach as in Exercise A-1. However, when the user types −99, the program should also print out the total of all nights stayed (TOTNIGHTS) and the total of all charges (TOTCHARGE) on two separate lines of the screen.

Exercise A-3

This exercise is a little more difficult but you may enjoy having a go at it.

An employee receives £2.35 for all hours worked up to 40. The *next* 10 hours, if any, are paid at £3.35 per hour, and the remainder at £4.35. Write a program called WAGES that will print out hours worked and pay for the employee. Use variables called HRS and PAY.

Unit 5 Text and character strings

Up to now the programs we have looked at have dealt with *numbers* only. For example: WRITELN statements have printed out the results of arithmetic calculations; assignment statements have assigned numbers to variables; and IF statements have compared one number to another.

Now we pass on to *text*. When the following statement:

    WRITELN ('TAX RATE');

is executed, the text TAX RATE will be printed on the screen. The new feature here is the quotation marks (or quotes). All text or characters enclosed by single quotes are printed out literally as they stand, including spaces. The quotes themselves are not printed.

A common place to print text is before a READ statement. For example:

    WRITELN ('TYPE EXCHANGE RATE');
    READ (EXRATE);

will cause the following to appear on the screen:

    TYPE EXCHANGE RATE

with the program waiting for input from the user. The printed text now makes it clear what the user is expected to type in.

◑ Qu 5.1 Write the next two lines of the program fragment above, to allow the user to type in the number of dollars to be exchanged. The program should print out the text TYPE NUMBER OF DOLLARS. Use the variable DOLLARS.

A WRITELN statement can include both text and variables, as in:

WRITELN ('KILOGRAMS REMAINING =', KILOS);

where KILOS is a variable representing the number of kilograms remaining. If KILOS has the value of 67 when this WRITELN statement is executed, the following will appear on the screen:

KILOGRAMS REMAINING = 67

The comma in the WRITELN statement acts just as before, specifying output is to be printed across the screen. (The number of spaces between the equals sign and the number 67 will vary with the computer used and with any formatting information included in the statement, see page 114.)

So text is used to make a program more understandable to the user. Below is another example. Note that in this example, the text has been written in lower case letters, which can make a program and its output more readable. In this book we will sometimes use lower case for text and assume the resulting output is in lower case. However, some small computers do not provide lower case letters, so all the program must be typed in upper case.

```
PROGRAM PETROL (INPUT, OUTPUT);
VAR       MILES, GALS: REAL;
BEGIN
   WRITELN ('Type distance in miles');
   READ (MILES);
   WRITELN ('Type gallons used');
   READ (GALS);
   WRITELN ('Miles-per-gallon =', MILES / GALS);
END.
```

◑ Qu 5.2   Assume the above program PETROL is running on a computer and the user types in a mileage of 120 and gallons used as 4. What output will be displayed on the screen after the program is run (give all five lines)?

◑ Qu 5.3   In a program that prints out bills, the variable DUE stands for amount due. Write a statement that will print out the text AMOUNT DUE.... followed on the same line by the value of the amount due.

Up to now in this Unit we have talked about *text*. However, a more common and accurate term is *character string*. The reason should become clear after the use of the term *character* in computer programming is explained.

A character refers not only to the 26 alphabetic letters (A to Z), but also to the ten digits (0 to 9) and to punctuation and mathematical symbols such as:

comma	,
hyphen	-
asterisk	*
percentage	%
pound sign	£
plus	+
space	

so even a space or a blank is regarded as a character. The following *string* of characters, then, contains 11 characters including two spaces:

A B-4/7 2,£

When any character string is included between quotes in a WRITELN statement, that character is printed out exactly as it stands. No attempt is made to interpret the characters as variables or to perform arithmetic on the digits.

◑ Qu 5.4 What will be printed out when each of the following statements is executed?

(a) WRITELN ('VAT AT 15%');
(b) WRITELN ('A');
(c) WRITELN ('Price ', '£18');
(d) WRITELN ('4 + 2 =', 4 + 2);

Ans 5.1 WRITELN ('TYPE NUMBER OF DOLLARS');
READ (DOLLARS);

Spaces are often included in WRITELN statements. For example:

WRITELN ('   DISTANCE   ', MILES);

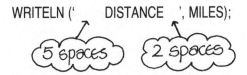

When printed, the word DISTANCE will be indented by five spaces and there will be two spaces before the equals sign.

When writing by hand, the inclusion of spaces is not always clear. If spacing is important, the symbol △ can be used to show a space:

WRITELN ('△△△△△DISTANCE△△=', MILES);

Of course, when actually typing in the program on a computer, the △ symbol is not used.

◐ Qu 5.5   A program uses the variable TAX to represent tax. Write a statement that will print out the text TAX AT 10% followed on the same line by the value of the tax. Indent the word tax by four spaces and leave two spaces on either side of the word AT. Use the symbol △ to indicate spaces.

Ans 5.2   Type distance in miles
          120
          Type gallons used
          4
          Miles-per-gallon = 30

Ans 5.3   WRITELN ('AMOUNT DUE. . . .', DUE);

Character variables   Up to now all variables we have used have represented real or integer numbers. These are called *numeric* variables (and were introduced in Unit 2, although the term numeric was not used there). Variables can also be used to represent characters. These are called *character* variables. A character variable can represent a single character only (we will come to variables that represent strings of two or more characters later).

In the VAR declaration, numeric variables must be declared as type REAL or INTEGER. Character variables must be declared as type CHAR. For example:

>   VAR SYMBOL, GRADE: CHAR;

declares the variables SYMBOL and GRADE as character variables.

We can now write assignment statements such as the following. Note the character value must be enclosed in quotes:

>   SYMBOL := 'A';
>   SYMBOL :='£';
>   SYMBOL := ' ';

The last statement gives SYMBOL the value of one space.

We can also write IF statements, again with the character value enclosed in quotes:

>   IF GRADE = 'A' THEN WRITELN ('EXCELLENT');
>   IF GRADE = 'B' THEN WRITELN ('GOOD');
>   IF GRADE = 'C' THEN WRITELN ('AVERAGE');

Computers can rank characters as well as numbers, for example A may be low and Z may be high. Hence we could write:

>   IF GRADE <= 'C' THEN WRITELN ('PASSED');

Ans 5.4   (a) VAT AT 15%
          (b) A
          (c) Price £18
          (d) 4 + 2 = 6

The next program provides a simple example of character manipulation. (Do not attempt to run this program until you have read down to Qu 5.8.)

```
PROGRAM REORDER (INPUT, OUTPUT);
VAR       CH1, CH2, CH3, CH4: CHAR;
BEGIN
   READ (CH1, CH2, CH3, CH4);
   WRITELN (CH4, CH3, CH2, CH1);
END.
```

The following are examples of input and corresponding output for this program. Remember a character variable can hold only one character.

Input	Output
123+	+321
E/12	21/E
ABCD	DCBA
AB D	D BA

◗ **Qu 5.6** Suppose the REORDER program is running and the last example of input given above has been typed in. After the READ statement has been executed, what is the value of (a) CH2, and (b) CH3?

◗ **Qu 5.7** Write a statement that assigns the value 8 to a character variable called DIGIT.

Unfortunately, reading character values is not as straightforward as reading numeric values. A later program in this Unit will require a user to answer a question by typing Y or N (for yes or no). Suppose by accident or design the user types one or more spaces before this answer:

ΔY

space before the answer

Ans 5.5   WRITELN ('ΔΔΔΔTAXΔΔATΔΔ10%', TAX);

With a character variable, the READ statement reads each individual character in the input stream in turn, including spaces. So if the first character is a space, this would be read instead of the Y, causing an error.

A related and more common problem concerns the action of the RETURN key (which causes a carriage return, see the Appendix page 113). When this key is pressed, it may insert a space into the input stream. Hence if a character READ occurs after the RETURN key has been pressed, a space could be read in error. Finally, in some versions of Pascal, the very first character in the input stream is always a space (due to a carriage return), which will cause an error if the first READ statement in a program reads a character.

One technique for dealing with these problems is to skip over any leading spaces. This can be done by using loops such as the one shown in the following fragment (where ANSWER is a character variable):

```
REPEAT
   READ (ANSWER);
UNTIL ANSWER <> ' ';
IF ANSWER = 'Y' THEN . . .
```

The REPEAT statement is executed repeatedly until a character is read that is not a space.

Below is the main body of the REORDER program (page 55), rewritten to skip over any leading spaces before the first data character:

```
BEGIN
   REPEAT
      READ (CH1);
   UNTIL CH1 <> ' ';
   READ (CH2, CH3, CH4);
   WRITELN (CH4, CH3, CH2, CH1);
END.
```

The program will now always produce the output from the corresponding input shown on page 55, even with versions of Pascal where the first character in the input stream is always a space.

● Qu 5.8   Write a program called SURNAME that first prints out the text PLEASE TYPE YOUR SURNAME. When the user has typed his surname, the program should print out only the first letter of the surname. Use a variable called CH and allow for leading spaces in the input stream.

The technique of skipping spaces cannot be used if the input data contains genuine spaces that need to be read (for example, the first data character to be read by the REORDER program cannot now be a space). In such cases, other techniques must be used (for example, see the Appendix, page 114). But skipping spaces can be used in the great majority of cases, and will be used in this book where there is a possibility of leading spaces causing an error, including spaces introduced by the RETURN key.

With numeric variables, the need to skip spaces never arises. Here the computer is looking *only* for numeric values and will automatically skip spaces. Similarly, the computer recognizes the end of a numeric value when it reads a space. This is why we said in Unit 3 that numeric values typed in by the user must be followed by at least one space (or by pressing RETURN). (Note: Some versions of Pascal recognize the end of a numeric value when any non-numeric character is read.)

The next program contains both numeric and character variables. The program calculates petrol charges, given a price of £1.90 a gallon. A surcharge of £0.5 is added if payment is not in cash. The REPEAT loop that skips spaces before reading the ANSWER to the cash payment question has been written on one line:

```
PROGRAM PETBILL (INPUT, OUTPUT);
VAR      GALS, CHARGE: INTEGER;
         ANSWER      : CHAR;
BEGIN
   WRITELN ('Type number of gallons');
   READ (GALS);
   WRITELN ('Is payment by cash? Y or N');
   REPEAT READ (ANSWER) UNTIL ANSWER <> ' ';
   CHARGE := GALS * 1.90;
   WRITELN ('Petrol charge = ', CHARGE);
   IF ANSWER = 'N' THEN
     BEGIN WRITELN ('Surcharge = 0.5');
           WRITELN ('Total charge = ', CHARGE + 0.5);
     END;
END.
```

Ans 5.6   (a) B   (b) a space

Ans 5.7   DIGIT := '8';
Did you remember the quotes?

The following shows some possible responses typed in by the user when this program is running:

Type number of gallons
10 ←———————————
Is payment by cash? Y or N
N ←———————————

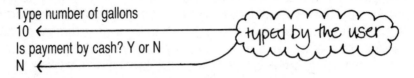

If pressing the RETURN key after typing in the number of gallons introduces a space into the input stream, no error is caused.

◐   Qu 5.9   If the program PETBILL is running and the user types in the responses shown above, what is then printed out?

String variables   Character variables can represent only a single character. String variables can represent a string of one or more characters. Some versions of Pascal, including UCSD Pascal, provide a STRING type for declaring string variables, for example:

    VAR NAME, ADDRESS, DATE: STRING;

Given this VAR declaration we can write statements such as:

    NAME := 'M. J. OATEY';
    ADDRESS := '103, BOROUGH RD., LONDON SE1.';
    IF DATE = '17/11/60' THEN WRITELN ('BIRTHDAY WINNER');

again enclosing the string values in quotes.

Ans 5.8   PROGRAM SURNAME (INPUT, OUTPUT);
           VAR   CH: CHAR;
           BEGIN
             WRITELN ('PLEASE TYPE YOUR SURNAME');
             REPEAT
               READ (CH);
             UNTIL CH <> ' ';
             WRITELN (CH);
           END.

Some versions of Pascal, including Standard Pascal, do not provide a STRING type and a different technique must be used to declare and use string variables. Therefore note the next program will not run as it stands in Standard Pascal, but will run in UCSD Pascal.

```
PROGRAM GREETING (INPUT, OUTPUT);
VAR        NAME: STRING;
BEGIN
   WRITELN ('PLEASE TYPE YOUR FIRST NAME');
   READ (NAME);
   WRITELN ('HELLO ', NAME);
END.
```

◖ Qu 5.10   Suppose the program GREETING is running and a user called Susy types in her name (in upper case). What is then printed out by the computer?

◖ Qu 5.11   A program that calculates car hire charges uses the following variables:

NAME   customer's name
REG   car registration number (e.g. FUV 727A)
MILES miles driven
RATE   rate per mile

Write a VAR declaration for the program. (Assume the STRING type is provided.)

With versions of Pascal that do not provide a STRING type, string variables must be declared and used by means of a more complex technique involving *arrays*. The technique is introduced in Unit 8 (page 100) but not covered in detail. Therefore, unless otherwise stated, string variables are not used in further programs in this book.

Note: If you do have access to a computer that provides the STRING type, you should refer to the reference manual for further details of its use.

Numeric and string values   It is important to distinguish clearly between numeric and string values (a character value being a special type of string value that can contain only one character). Arithmetic can be carried out only on numeric values and, to allow for this, numeric values are treated in the computer in a different way to string values.

A string value can include any characters. A numeric value can include only digits, a decimal point, and a plus or minus sign; if any other characters are included, the value becomes a string value. Here are some examples:

Numeric values	*String values*
20000	20,000
+23	+ 23
67.5	£67.5
	FUV 727A

In statements, string values must be enclosed in quotes; numeric values must not be enclosed in quotes.

In READ and assignment statements, numeric variables must be given numeric values only. In conditions in IF statements (and in REPEAT and WHILE statements), numeric variables must be compared to numeric values only. Therefore assuming VAR1 is a numeric variable, the following statements are *illegal*:

    VAR1 := 33%;
    VAR1 := £750;
    IF VAR1 = 20P THEN WRITELN ('Correct');

String values must be enclosed in quotes in statements. Therefore assuming VAR2 is a character or string variable, the following statements are *illegal*:

    VAR2 := A;
    VAR2 := %;
    IF VAR2 = P THEN WRITELN ('Correct');
    WRITELN (33%);

Ans 5.9   Petrol charges = 19.0
          Surcharge = 0.5
          Total charge = 19.5

String values cannot be used in arithmetic. Therefore the following statements are *illegal*:

```
RESULT := VAR1 – VAR2;
WRITELN (VAR2 * 5);
```

Finally, note in particular that a value such as 256 can be treated as either a numeric value or a string value: it could be a numeric value that can be used in arithmetic; or it could be a string value consisting of three characters (the digits 2, 5, and 6). Thus both the following statements are possible:

```
VAR1 := 256;
VAR2 := '256';
```

◗ Qu 5.12 Assuming VAR1 is a numeric variable and VAR2 is a character variable, identify any errors in the following statements:

```
(a)  VAR1 := 105,000;
(b)  VAR2 := Q;
(c)  VAR2 := '3';
(d)  VAR1 := '250';
(e)  VAR1 := −2.45;
(f)  VAR2 := ' ';
(g)  WRITELN (VAR1, VAR2);
(h)  WRITELN (VAR2 / 5);
(i)  IF VAR2 = M THEN WRITELN ('STOP');
(k)  WRITELN (£500000);
```

Ans 5.10 HELLO SUSY

Ans 5.11 VAR NAME, REG: STRING:
　　　　　　MILES, RATE: REAL;

Summary (Unit 5)

○ A *character* can be a letter, a digit, a punctuation mark, a mathematical symbol, or a space. A *character string* is a continuous string of such characters.

○ In a WRITELN statement, any character string enclosed by single quotes is printed exactly as it stands. The quotes are not printed.

○ *Numeric* variables represent real and integer numbers (see Unit 2). *Character* variables represent single characters. *String* variables represent character strings.

○ Character variables are declared as type CHAR. In some versions of Pascal, including UCSD, string variables can be declared as type STRING. Other versions of Pascal, including Standard, do not provide a STRING type and require a more complex technique for declaring and using string variables.

○ Rules for using numeric and string values are:

numeric values	*string values*
can include only digits, a decimal point, and a plus or minus sign	can include any characters
must not be enclosed in quotes	must be enclosed in single quotes in statements
can be assigned only to numeric variables	can be assigned only to string and character variables
can be used in arithmetic	cannot be used in arithmetic

Further questions

5.13   A licence is subject to a surcharge. If the licence expires in October, November, or December, the surcharge is £55. Otherwise it is £35. Write a program called LICENCE that will first print the following text TYPE MONTH NUMBER (1 TO 12). When the user has typed in the number of the month, the program should display the value of the surcharge including the £ sign. Use the variable MONTH for month.

5.14   Wine costs £2.45 a bottle. If delivery is required, there is a fixed charge of £3 irrespective of the number of bottles. Write a program that will ask the user to type in the number of bottles and whether delivery is required; the response to the delivery question should be Y for yes and N for no (allow for leading spaces). The program should print out the text WINE CHARGES followed on the same line by the total charge. Then the program should ask the user to type in a number of bottles again, and so on until −99 is typed in. Call the program WINE and use variables called BOTTLES, ANSWER, and CHARGE.

5.15   Write a program that counts and prints out the number of occurrences of the letter A and of the letter B in a sentence. Use variables called CH, ACOUNT, and BCOUNT. Assume the sentence ends with a full stop. Call the program AB.

Ans 5.12   (a) comma is illegal (in a numeric value)

          (b) Q must be enclosed by quotes (since it is a string value)

          (c) no errors

          (d) quotes must not be used (since VAR1 is a numeric variable)

          (e) no errors

          (f) no errors

          (g) no errors

          (h) VAR2 cannot be used in arithmetic (since it is a character variable)

          (i) M must be enclosed by quotes (since it is a string value)

          (k) £500000 must be enclosed by quotes (since it is a string value)

Unit 6 Procedures

Procedures allow programs to be broken down into smaller sections, which can make the programs easier to write, to read, and to modify.

The following program contains a procedure. This program analyses answers to a question, for example in a survey, and prints out the number of "yes" answers (TOTYES). The end of data marker is F (for Finish).

```
PROGRAM ANALYSIS (INPUT, OUTPUT);
VAR      ANS: CHAR;
             TOTYES: INTEGER;

PROCEDURE SKIPREAD;
BEGIN
  REPEAT
    READ (ANS);                    ← procedure
  UNTIL ANS <> ' ';
END;

BEGIN
  TOTYES := 0;
  SKIPREAD;  ←
  WHILE ANS <> 'F' DO
    BEGIN
      IF ANS = 'Y'                 procedure calls
      THEN TOTYES := TOTYES + 1;
      SKIPREAD;  ←
    END;
  WRITELN (TOTYES);
END.
```

The program contains a procedure called SKIPREAD, which *skips* leading spaces and *reads* an answer. Procedures are given names in the same way that programs are named. We could have used a name such as SKIPSPACESREAD or SKIPRD or SKIPREADANS.

The SKIPREAD procedure is followed by the main program, which contains two *calls* to the procedure. A procedure is called by stating its name and, when called, all the statements in the procedure are executed. So the above program could be re-written without a procedure by inserting the statement:

```
REPEAT
  READ (ANS);
UNTIL ANS <> ' ';
```

in the two places where SKIPREAD now occurs. A procedure can be thought of as a means of creating a new Pascal statement. Here we have effectively created a statement called SKIPREAD.

The advantages of the procedure here are: the name SKIPREAD is more readable than the REPEAT statement; the REPEAT statement is written once rather than twice; and the main program becomes less cluttered. Of course, this program is short and simple, and the advantages of using a procedure are not very great. But as programs become longer and more complex, the need for procedures increases.

◑ Qu 6.1 Turn to the program in Exercise B-1 (page 77), which contains a procedure. (a) What is the name of the procedure? (b) How often is it called?

The lines enclosed by the bracket in the program ANALYSIS above form a *procedure declaration*. The simplest general format of a procedure declaration is:

```
PROCEDURE procedure-name;
BEGIN
  statement-sequence;
END;
```

where the *statement-sequence* contains one or more statements separated by semicolons. Notice the END statement is followed by a semicolon, not a full stop (a full stop occurs at the end of the whole program). A procedure must be declared before it can be called.

A program can contain any number of procedures, but for the present we will consider programs that contain just one procedure.

The next example involves a "data validation" sequence. Data validation is the process of testing data to see if it contains errors or falls within reasonable limits. Suppose a program requests a user to type in a month using numbers 1 to 12 (as in Qu 5.13). If a number larger than 12 is typed, it must be wrong. We can "trap" this error by a sequence such as:

```
REPEAT
   READ (MONTH);
   IF MONTH > 12
      THEN WRITELN ('NUMBER EXCEEDS 12. PLEASE RE-TYPE');
UNTIL MONTH <= 12;
```

◑ **Qu 6.2**   Write a declaration for a procedure called READMONTH that contains the above statements.

The variable MONTH in the above procedure (in Qu 6.2) would be declared at the beginning of the program in the usual way, and can be used in both the main program and the procedure. However, if a variable is to be used *only* in a procedure, it can be declared in that procedure. Such variables are called *local* variables, and are declared in a VAR declaration after the procedure heading. For example:

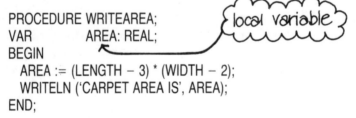

```
PROCEDURE WRITEAREA;                    local variable
VAR        AREA: REAL;
BEGIN
   AREA := (LENGTH – 3) * (WIDTH – 2);
   WRITELN ('CARPET AREA IS', AREA);
END;
```

AREA is a local variable and is not used in the main program. LENGTH and WIDTH are used in the main program as well as the procedure and are said to be *global* variables; they would be declared at the beginning of the program. AREA could also be declared as a global variable at the beginning of the program, but declaring it as a local variable can again make the program more readable. In addition, using local variables is more efficient for the computer and can reduce errors due to duplicate variable names (since local variables in different procedures can have the same name, though this is not a practice to be encouraged).

The next example is a procedure for exchanging the values of two variables (the procedure will be needed in Unit 8 in a program for sorting). The following sequence exchanges the values of NUM1 and NUM2, using a variable called STORE to temporarily hold the value of NUM1:

```
STORE := NUM1;
NUM1  := NUM2;
NUM2  := STORE;
```

◐ **Qu 6.3**   Write a declaration for a procedure called SWAP that contains the above three statements. Declare STORE as a local variable of type REAL.

Parameters

The power and usefulness of procedures can be greatly increased by the use of *parameters*. This is a major topic in Pascal, but is relatively complex and is only introduced here without going into detail.

Parameters allow the action of a procedure to be made general. For example, the SWAP procedure in Qu 6.3 can exchange only the values of two specific variables (NUM1 and NUM2), whereas the following procedure can exchange the values of *any* two variables. This procedure uses two parameters X and Y, which are declared between brackets *in* the procedure heading:

```
PROCEDURE SWAP (VAR X, Y: REAL);        parameters
VAR          STORE: REAL;
BEGIN
  STORE := X;
  X      := Y;
  Y      := STORE;
END;
```

Ans 6.1   (a) OVERBOOKED   (b) once

Now the procedure call to exchange NUM1 and NUM2 becomes:

    SWAP (NUM1, NUM2);

When the procedure is executed, NUM1 replaces X and NUM2 replaces Y, and therefore the result is the same as before. However, we can also write:

    SWAP (NUM3, NUM4);

when NUM3 replaces X and NUM4 replaces Y. Similarly we can write:

    SWAP (NUM1, NUM4);
    SWAP (A, B);
    SWAP (FIRST, LAST);

The corresponding variable and parameter must both be declared as the same type. So in the above examples, NUM1, NUM4, A, B, FIRST, and LAST must all have been declared as type REAL.

The parameters in the procedure heading are known as *formal* parameters. So, with parameters, the general format of the procedure heading becomes:

    PROCEDURE *procedure-name* (VAR *formal-parameter-declaration*);

where *formal-parameter-declaration* is a list of one or more variables declared in the same way as in a VAR declaration (including specifying the type, such as REAL or CHAR). Some parameters are not preceded by the word VAR, for reasons beyond the scope of this book.

The parameters in the procedure call are known as *actual* parameters. So, with parameters, the general format of the procedure call becomes:

    procedure-name (*actual-parameters*);

Ans 6.2   PROCEDURE READMONTH;
          BEGIN
            REPEAT
              READ (MONTH);
              IF MONTH > 12
              THEN WRITELN ('NUMBER EXCEEDS 12. PLEASE RE-TYPE');
            UNTIL MONTH <= 12;
          END;

where *actual-parameters* is a list of one or more parameters separated by commas.

When a procedure is called, the actual parameters replace the formal parameters. Replacement is done in order: the first actual parameter replaces the first formal parameter and so on. There must be the same number of formal and actual parameters and, as stated above, the corresponding parameters must be of the same type.

◐ Qu 6.4   A procedure called ORDER re-assigns the values of four integer variables such that the first variable holds the highest value, the second variable holds the second highest value, and so on. The procedure uses formal parameters called W, X, Y, and Z. (a) Write a heading for the procedure. (b) Write a call to the procedure using actual parameters NUM1, NUM2, NUM3, and NUM4.

◐ Qu 6.5   Turn to the program ANALYSIS on page 64. (a) Rewrite the procedure SKIPREAD using a formal parameter called CH. (b) Rewrite a procedure call.

Notice that when parameters are used, procedure calls become more self-explanatory. Thus with the call:

SKIPREAD (ANS);

you can tell at a glance that the variable ANS is being read. Using parameters to improve the readability of a program in this way is considered to be good programming "style".

We have seen that parameters generalize the action of a procedure by making the procedure independent of the specific variables used in the main program. Indeed, a "parameterized" procedure is independent of any program so, for example, the parameterized procedures SKIPREAD and SWAP could be inserted into other programs. Thus a user can build up a "library" of procedures for use in programs as required, avoiding the need to write (and test) the procedures for each separate program. The more complex the procedures, the greater the advantage.

```
Ans 6.3   PROCEDURE SWAP;
           VAR          STORE: REAL;
           BEGIN
             STORE := NUM1;
             NUM1  := NUM2;
             NUM2  := STORE;
           END;
```

The purpose of this section has been to introduce you to parameters and to emphasize their advantages. It is beyond the scope of a short course to give all the rules governing their use or to provide detailed practice, and we will not introduce any more new parameterized procedures in this book; however, we will make some further use of the parameterized SWAP and SKIPREAD procedures given above. If you continue with Pascal, you should make a full study of parameters a high priority.

Functions   Functions are similar to procedures and have the same objectives, including making a program more readable and avoiding duplication of effort. Functions can be written by the user like procedures, with a heading starting with the word FUNCTION instead of PROCEDURE. We will not go into further details but simply note that functions can be more convenient than procedures when just one result is produced.

In addition to "user-written" functions, Pascal provides some predefined "standard" functions, which have been written for you. For example, there are standard functions to find squares, square roots, sines, cosines, and truncated and rounded values.

Again if you continue with Pascal, you should investigate both user-written and standard functions. Any comprehensive book on Pascal will list the standard functions available.

Blocks   Note: All general references to procedures in this section also refer to user-written functions.

A program can contain any number of procedures. And a procedure can itself contain other procedures, that is, procedures can be nested. For example, the program in Exercise C-2 (page 107) contains a procedure called SWAP that is nested in another procedure called SORTUP. A procedure can call other procedures, and can even call itself (a process known as recursion).

A *block* consists of all components except the heading of a program or procedure. Up to Unit 6 in this book, all programs have contained one block. Up to this section in Unit 6, we have considered programs that contain two blocks: a main program block and a procedure block. Now the program in Exercise C-2 contains three blocks. A Pascal program, then, contains one or more blocks some of which are nested in others.

When a block is nested in another block, any variables declared in the outer block can be used in the inner block. Such variables declared in an outer block are said to be global to an inner block. Variables declared at the beginning of a program are said to be global (without qualification); such variables are of course global to every block in the program. Variables declared at the beginning of a block are said to be local to that block and can be used only within the block.

◑ Qu 6.6   Turn to the program in Exercise C-2 (page 107). (Treat LIST as an ordinary variable for the purposes of this question.) State variables that are:

(a) global
(b) global to the block headed SWAP
(c) local to the block headed SORTUP

A programming language that uses blocks is said to be block-structured. Block-structured languages help you to write well organized programs. You should be starting to appreciate that more complicated programs can be much easier to follow when procedures are used. But note that procedures can be overused, resulting in fragmented programs that are again difficult to follow because they are broken up too much; the extent to which a program is broken down into smaller blocks is a matter of judgement. The ideas behind programming strategy are explained further in the Postscript (page 109).

Ans 6.4   (a) PROCEDURE ORDER (VAR W, X, Y, Z: INTEGER);
          (b) ORDER (NUM1, NUM2, NUM3, NUM4);

Ans 6.5   (a) PROCEDURE SKIPREAD (VAR CH: CHAR);
              BEGIN
                REPEAT
                  READ (CH);
                UNTIL CH <> ' ';
              END;
          (b) SKIPREAD (ANS);

Comments in programs

This is a convenient point to introduce the use of comments in programs. Comments are included in programs solely for the benefit of the programmer and are ignored by the computer when a program is run. The start of a comment is shown by the symbols (* and the finish of a comment by the symbols *), for example:

(* THIS IS A COMMENT *)

In some versions of Pascal, comments are enclosed by curly brackets (without asterisks).

The next program contains comments:

```
PROGRAM PERCENT (INPUT, OUTPUT);
(* PROGRAM TO FIND 15% OF A NUMBER TYPED IN BY A USER *)
VAR     NUM: REAL;              (* NUM CONTAINS A NUMBER TYPED IN *)
BEGIN
   READ (NUM);
   WHILE NUM <> −1 DO          (* END OF DATA MARKER IS −1 *)
     BEGIN
        WRITELN (NUM * 0.15);    (* PRINT OUT 15% OF THE NUMBER *)
        READ (NUM);
     END;
END.
```

Comments become important with longer or more complex programs, especially if they are to be read by someone else or are to be revised later. Imagine trying to follow a program hundreds or thousands of lines long written by someone else, or even written by yourself six months earlier. Most professional computer installations have strict rules about including comments in programs (which is part of a process called *documenting* a program).

However, with short programs that are to be used only by the programmer and not kept, comments become less important. Indeed they can clutter up a short simple program unnecessarily. For this reason, comments have not been introduced until here.

In the next program called HIGHEST, comments have been written in lower case letters so they stand out more clearly. Again, some small microcomputers may not provide lower case letters, so upper case must be used as in the previous program PERCENT.

Now follow through the program HIGHEST with the help of the comments.

```
PROGRAM HIGHEST (INPUT, OUTPUT);
(* program to find the highest of a series of letters typed in by the user (A is low, Z is high) *)
VAR  LETTER,           (* to contain each letter typed in *)
         HI         : CHAR;   (* to contain the highest letter *)

PROCEDURE SKIPREAD (VAR CH: CHAR);
(* skips leading spaces and reads a letter *)
BEGIN
   REPEAT
      READ (CH);
   UNTIL CH <> ' ';
END;

BEGIN
   WRITELN ('Type in letters (type * to finish)');
   SKIPREAD (LETTER);
   (* place the first letter into HI *)
   HI := LETTER;
   WHILE LETTER <> '*' DO
      BEGIN
         (* place the highest letter so far into HI *)
         IF LETTER > HI THEN HI := LETTER;
         SKIPREAD (LETTER);
      END;
   (* HI now contains the highest letter *)
   WRITELN ('Highest letter = ', HI);
END.
```

◗   Qu 6.7   Suppose during a run of the program HIGHEST, the user types the letters G, A, T, K, W, and then an asterisk.

    (a) State the value of HI just before the first execution of the WHILE loop
    (b) State the value of HI just before the last execution of the WHILE loop
    (c) What is printed out after the user has typed the asterisk?

Ans 6.6   (a) U, LIST
       (b) U, LIST, POSN
       (c) POSN

Summary (Unit 6)

○ Procedures allow a program to be broken down into sections, which can make the program easier to write, read, and modify. In effect, procedures allow a programmer to create his own statements.

○ A general format of a procedure declaration is:

```
PROCEDURE procedure-name;
VAR local-variable-declaration;
BEGIN
    statement-sequence;
END;
```

Local variables can be used only within the procedure, and are declared in the same form as *global* variables are declared at the beginning of the program.

○ Procedures are called by stating the name. A procedure must be declared before it can be called.

○ *Parameters* make a procedure independent of variable names used in other parts of a program. Using parameters can avoid duplication of effort and can make a program more readable.

○ Functions are similar to procedures but can be more convenient when just one result is produced. Pascal also provides some predefined standard functions.

○ All components except the heading of a program or procedure or function make up a *block*. A program can contain any number of blocks, and blocks can be nested in other blocks. Variables declared in an outer block can be used in an inner block and are said to be global to the inner block.

○ Comments are included in programs for the benefit of the programmer and are ignored by the computer when a program is run. Comments must be enclosed by the symbols (* and *) or by curly brackets, depending on the version of Pascal.

Further questions

6.8 A program requires a user to type in a weekday using numbers 1 to 5. Write a procedure called READAY that displays the text:

Type weekday number (Mon = 1, Fri = 5)

The procedure should validate the input and request the user to retype any number over 5. Assume a global variable called DAY has been declared as type INTEGER.

6.9 A program called TIME, which reads in hours and minutes, has the following statements in the main program:

```
READ (HRS);
WHILE HRS <> −9 DO
   BEGIN
      READ (MINS);
      PRINTEXCESS;
      READ (HRS);
   END;
```

PRINTEXCESS is a procedure that converts the hours and minutes into minutes, and then prints TIME EXCESS if time exceeds 150 minutes or prints TIME NORMAL if time is 150 minutes or less. The procedure uses a local variable called MINUTES. Write the complete program.

6.10 Write a program called LOWEST to find the lowest of a series of positive numbers typed in by the user. Use −9 as the end of data marker, and use variables called NUM and LOW. The program should print out suitable text for the user. Insert comments in the program where appropriate.

Ans 6.7 (a) G
(b) T
(c) Highest letter = W

Exercises B

Exercise B-1

The program opposite illustrates the use of computers to reserve seats on aircraft. Reservations could be made by, for example, a receptionist at an airport or a travel agent.

Suppose the program is running and the following is being displayed on the screen:

> Flight AB24:   7 seats available
> Please type number of seats required

with the program waiting for the receptionist to type in a number. What then appears on the screen if the receptionist types in (a) 9, (b) 7, and (c) 5?

Comments   A more complex program would deal with many flights (the receptionist would also be asked to type in the flight number) and with cancellations. In addition, details of passengers may be recorded in a data file. (Files are briefly explained in the Postscript.)

Bookings are usually made from several locations: airports, stations, travel agents, etc. Each location would have a computer terminal (consisting of a video screen and keyboard) linked to a central computer. The central computer runs the program and updates the seats available (SEATS). So all locations have immediate access to the number of seats available and no user can overbook the flight.

```
PROGRAM RESERVATIONS (INPUT, OUTPUT);
(* seat reservations for flight AB24 *)

VAR  SEATS,                  (* seats available *)
     NUMREQ: INTEGER;        (* number of seats required at each booking *)

PROCEDURE OVERBOOKED;
(* seats required exceeds seats available *)
BEGIN
  REPEAT
    WRITELN ('There are only ', SEATS, ' seats available');
    WRITELN ('Please retype number required');
    READ (NUMREQ);
  UNTIL NUMREQ <= SEATS;
END;

BEGIN (* main program *)
  SEATS := 152;              (* aircraft capacity is 152 seats *)

  REPEAT (* until all seats booked *)
    WRITELN ('Flight AB24:   ', SEATS, ' seats available');
    WRITELN ('Please type number of seats required');
    READ (NUMREQ);
    IF NUMREQ > SEATS THEN OVERBOOKED;

    (* confirm booking and update seats available *)
    WRITELN (NUMREQ, ' seats booked. Thank you');
    SEATS := SEATS - NUMREQ;
  UNTIL SEATS = 0;

  (* flight full *)
  WRITELN ('Flight AB24 fully booked');
END.
```

Exercise B-2

The program opposite illustrates the use of computers to analyze questionnaires or census data. The program analyzes one question, which can have replies of yes (Y), no (N), or don't know (D).

Note that the second and sixth lines of the main program contain more than one statement. Pascal statements can be laid out in any way, across or down the screen, provided they are separated by semicolons.

In a more complete program, the input data would be validated to detect errors. Thus sex must be M or F, and the reply must be Y, N, or D. Age could be validated for reasonable limits, say over 15 and under 100.

Text is also needed giving instructions on typing in the data. However, this is quite straightforward since leading spaces will not cause any errors (because of the SKIPREAD procedure). The main requirement is that the age must be followed by at least one space or a carriage return. The end of data marker is an asterisk. Here are five example entries:

```
YM41
NF30
DM24
YM24
    *
```

Now answer these questions:

(a) Suppose the program is running and has already read hundreds of data entries. The totals accumulated so far are:

YES = 1550; NO = 1261; YESMALE = 735; YESOV40 = 1170

What will be printed out after the five example entries shown above have been typed in?

(b) Modify the program so that it will also print out the total under age 25 answering NO. (Use variable NOUN25.)

(c) Modify the program so that it will also print out the total number of people who answered the question. (Use variable TOTAL.)

```
PROGRAM QUESTIONNAIRE (INPUT, OUTPUT);  (* questionnaire analysis program *)
VAR  YES,                    (* total answering yes *)
     NO,                     (* total answering no *)
     YESMALE,                (* total of males answering yes *)
     YESOV40,                (* total over age 40 answering yes *)
     AGE     : INTEGER;      (* age of respondent *)
     SEX,                    (* M = male, F = female *)
     REPLY   : CHAR;         (* Y = yes, N = no, D = don't know *)

PROCEDURE YESREPLIES;  (* analyzes yes replies *)
BEGIN
   YES := YES + 1;
   IF AGE > 40 THEN YESOV40 := YESOV40 + 1;
   IF SEX = 'M' THEN YESMALE := YESMALE + 1;
END;

PROCEDURE NOREPLIES;   (* analyzes no replies *)
BEGIN
   NO := NO + 1;
END;

PROCEDURE SKIPREAD (VAR CH: CHAR);   (* skips leading spaces and reads a character *)
BEGIN
   REPEAT
     READ (CH);
   UNTIL CH <> ' ';
END;

BEGIN  (* main program *)
   YES := 0; NO := 0; YESOV40 := 0; YESMALE := 0;

   SKIPREAD (REPLY);
   WHILE REPLY <> '*' DO
     BEGIN
       SKIPREAD (SEX); READ (AGE);
       IF REPLY = 'Y' THEN YESREPLIES;
       IF REPLY = 'N' THEN NOREPLIES;
       SKIPREAD (REPLY);
     END;

   WRITELN ('Total answering Yes: ', YES);
   WRITELN ('Total answering No: ', NO);
   WRITELN ('Total of males answering Yes: ', YESMALE);
   WRITELN ('Total over age 40 answering Yes: ', YESOV40);
END.
```

Unit 7 FOR statements and loops

So far in this book we have set up loops using WHILE or REPEAT statements. This Unit looks at a third repetition statement that can be used for looping: the FOR statement. The FOR statement is used when the number of executions of a loop is known in advance (and is commonly used with arrays, which are introduced in Unit 8).

Here is an example:

```
FOR N := 1 TO 10 DO
   WRITELN (N);
```

which will print out all integer numbers between 1 and 10 inclusive. The first line beginning with FOR gives the initial and final values of the variable N, which here are 1 and 10. On the first execution of the FOR statement, N is assigned the value 1. Hence the number 1 is printed by the WRITELN statement. On the second execution, N is assigned the value of 2 and hence the number 2 is printed out. On the third execution, N is assigned the value 3 and so on. When N reaches the final value of 10, the number 10 is printed but then the program drops through to the line following the WRITELN statement.

We could have used a REPEAT or WHILE statement instead of a FOR statement. For example, in Unit 2 we used a REPEAT statement in similar programs that print out a series of numbers, such as:

```
N := 1;
REPEAT
   WRITELN (N);
   N := N + 1;
UNTIL N > 10;
```

Both the FOR and REPEAT examples will produce the same result, but the FOR statement is easier to use (with less chance of making a mistake on the number of executions!). We can use the FOR statement here because we can readily see in advance the number of executions of the loop.

The FOR statement is thus a special case of the REPEAT or WHILE statement, and is more convenient when the number of executions of the loop can be specified in advance. A general format is:

> FOR *variable* := *initial* TO *final* DO
> *statement*;

where *statement* can be single or compound. The *variable* is assigned successive values between *initial* and *final* inclusive, and the *statement* is executed for each value.

Notice the assignment sign (:=) following the *variable*. Values are assigned in FOR statements as they are in assignment statements.

◑ Qu 7.1 Write a FOR statement that will print out all integer numbers between 100 and 999. Use a variable called N.

A complete program that includes a FOR statement is given below. Note the variable N is declared in the normal way (here as an integer variable).

```
PROGRAM TABLE (OUTPUT);
VAR        N: INTEGER;
BEGIN
   FOR N: = 1 TO 50 DO
      WRITELN (N, N * 5);
END.
```

The output of this program is a simple table:

1	5
2	10
3	15
.	.
.	.
50	250

The spacing between the two columns in the table will depend on the computer used and on any formatting information included in the WRITELN statement.

◐ Qu 7.2 Write a program that will print out a table converting pints to litres (to convert pints to litres multiply by 0.568). The table should start with 1 pint and end with 32 pints, increasing in one pint steps. Call the program PINTLITRE and use an integer variable called PINTS.

In the general format of the FOR statement, the word TO can be replaced by DOWNTO. Now the variable takes successive *decreasing* values between the initial and final values. For example:

```
FOR N := 10 DOWNTO 1 DO
    WRITELN (N * 2);
```

◐ Qu 7.3 What will be printed out by the above FOR statement, assuming N is an integer variable?

◐ Qu 7.4 Write a statement that prints a decreasing series of ages in steps of one year, starting at 65 and ending at 21. Use an integer variable called AGE.

FOR statements are used for the routine task of drawing lines on the screen. Such lines help to clarify the layout, for example to box a table or underline a heading. The following statement will produce a vertical line on the screen:

```
FOR N := 1 TO 22 DO
    WRITELN ('|');
```

vertical dash

The vertical line will cover 22 rows.

Notice here the variable N does not appear in the main body of the loop. N is used simply to count the number of executions of the loop, and hence N is sometimes called a *control variable*. This use of a FOR statement just to control a number of repetitions is very common.

The next statement will produce a horizontal line across an 80 character width screen:

```
FOR N := 1 TO 80 DO
   WRITE ('–');
```

We have used a WRITE statement here rather than a WRITELN statement, and this is a convenient point to explain the difference between the two statements. The difference depends on causing a carriage return, which in turn causes printing to begin at the beginning of the next line. The WRITELN statement always causes a carriage return after printing, therefore any subsequent WRITELN or WRITE statement starts printing at the beginning of the next line. The WRITE statement does not cause a carriage return, therefore any subsequent WRITELN or WRITE statement continues printing on the current line (if there is room).

The above FOR statement uses a WRITE statement and so prints 80 dashes *across* the screen. With a WRITELN statement, it would print 80 dashes down the screen, one dash at the beginning of each of 80 rows.

◗ Qu 7.5   Write a statement that will print a row of asterisks across a screen that is 40 characters wide. Use a variable called N.

A word of warning on the WRITE statement. With some versions of Pascal, the output of a WRITE statement is not actually printed until a WRITELN statement or the end of the program is reached. In complete programs in this book, a WRITELN statement or the end of the program always follows a WRITE statement, so there is no problem. But if you are running your own programs and find output from a WRITE statement is not printed when you require it, you must insert a "blank" WRITELN statement, as shown in the following fragment:

```
FOR N := 1 TO 80 DO
   WRITE ('–');
WRITELN;
```

Ans 7.1   FOR N := 100 TO 999 DO
              WRITELN (N);

A WRITELN statement always causes a carriage return. So a blank WRITELN following a WRITE statement causes any subsequent output to start at the beginning of the next line. A blank WRITELN following another WRITELN statement introduces a blank line into the output.

In the FOR statement examples so far, the initial and final values have been integer numbers. However, the initial and final values can be any expression that yields an integer value. For example:

```
X := 10;
FOR N := X TO X + 15 DO
    WRITELN (N);
```

will print all integer numbers between 10 and 25.

Note that the initial and final values cannot be real. It is not possible to specify steps from, say, 1 to 7.75.

◑ Qu 7.6 Write a program called SERIES that will print any series of increasing integer numbers. In response to the text TYPE FIRST NUMBER and TYPE LAST NUMBER, the user should be able to type the first and last numbers of the series. Use variables called FIRST, LAST, and N.

Ans 7.2
```
PROGRAM PINTLITRE (OUTPUT);
VAR      PINTS: INTEGER;
BEGIN
  FOR PINTS := 1 TO 32 DO
    WRITELN (PINTS, PINTS * 0.568);
END.
```

Ans 7.3 All even numbers between 20 and 2 inclusive (in decreasing order).

Ans 7.4
```
FOR AGE := 65 DOWNTO 21 DO
    WRITELN (AGE);
```

The next program contains a FOR loop with a compound statement:

```
PROGRAM DEMO (INPUT, OUTPUT);
VAR       SUM, LAST, N: INTEGER;
BEGIN
  SUM := 0;
  READ (LAST);
  FOR N := 1 TO LAST DO
    BEGIN
      SUM := SUM + N;
      WRITELN (N, SUM);
    END;
END.
```

◗ Qu 7.7 What is printed out by the program DEMO above, assuming LAST is given a value of 5?

A final general point on FOR statements is that the initial and final values can be characters. For example, assuming CH has been declared as type CHAR, we can write:

```
FOR CH := 'A' TO 'Z' DO
  WRITELN (CH);
```

with the initial and final values now enclosed in single quotes. On most computers, this statement will print out the alphabet. But on some computers, extra characters may be printed if they occur between A and Z in the character sequence of that computer; in this book we will assume no non-alphabetic characters come between A and Z.

◗ Qu 7.8 Write a FOR statement that will print all letters from G to A in reverse order. The letters should be printed across the screen on one row. Use a variable called CH.

Ans 7.5   FOR N := 1 TO 40 DO
              WRITE ('*');

Nested FOR statements   The body of a FOR loop can itself contain a FOR statement, that is, FOR statements can be nested. A good way of demonstrating nested FOR statements is to print out patterns such as:

```
1ABCDEFG
2ABCDEFG
3ABCDEFG
4ABCDEFG
5ABCDEFG
```

This pattern can be produced by the following fragment:

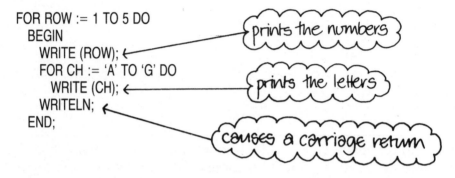

```
FOR ROW := 1 TO 5 DO
   BEGIN
      WRITE (ROW);          prints the numbers
      FOR CH := 'A' TO 'G' DO
         WRITE (CH);        prints the letters
      WRITELN;
   END;                     causes a carriage return
```

The WRITELN statement is included to cause a carriage return (otherwise printing would continue across the screen).
   Now consider this pattern:

```
ZYXWVUT*
ZYXWVUT*
ZYXWVUT*
ZYXWVUT*
```

Ans 7.6   PROGRAM SERIES (INPUT, OUTPUT);
         VAR   FIRST, LAST, N: INTEGER:
         BEGIN
            WRITELN ('TYPE FIRST NUMBER');
            READ (FIRST);
            WRITELN ('TYPE LAST NUMBER');
            READ (LAST);
            FOR N := FIRST TO LAST DO
               WRITELN (N);
         END.

○ Qu 7.9 Write a program called PATTERN that can print out the above pattern. Use a nested FOR statement and variables called ROW and CH.

In the next pattern, notice that the number of asterisks on a row corresponds to the row number (for example, row 4 contains four asterisks):

```
        *
        **
        ***
        ****
        *****
        ******
```

This pattern can be produced by the following fragment:

```
FOR ROW := 1 TO 6 DO
   BEGIN
      FOR N := 1 TO ROW DO
         WRITE ('*');
      WRITELN;
   END;
```

Note that on the first execution of the nested FOR statement, ROW has the value 1 and hence the third line becomes equivalent to:

```
FOR N := 1 TO 1 DO
```

This is quite legal and means the following WRITE statement is executed once only.

Ans 7.7   1   1
           2   3
           3   .   6
           4   10
           5   15

Ans 7.8   FOR CH := 'G' DOWNTO 'A' DO
              WRITE (CH);

It is also possible for a final value to be less than an initial value as in:

FOR N := 1 TO 0 DO

in which case the body of the loop is not executed at all. Reverse arguments apply when the DOWNTO option is used.

Qu 7.10   Write a program called PAT2 that will print out a 15 by 15 block of asterisks. Use variables called ROW and N.

The last program in this Unit contains two procedures. Notice how the procedures make the program much easier to read through.

```
PROGRAM PAT3 (OUTOUT);
VAR      N: INTEGER;

PROCEDURE PRINTROW;
VAR      R: INTEGER;
BEGIN
  FOR R := 1 TO 7 DO
    WRITE ('*');
END;

PROCEDURE PRINTCOLUMN;
VAR      C: INTEGER;
BEGIN
  FOR C := 1 TO 3 DO
    WRITELN ('    *');
END;

BEGIN (* main program *)
  FOR N := 1 TO 3 DO
    BEGIN
      PRINTROW;
      WRITELN;
      PRINTCOLUMN;
    END;
END.
```

prints an asterisk indented 3 spaces ← (pointing to WRITELN ('   *');)

Qu 7.11   Draw the pattern produced by the above program.

Summary (Unit 7)

○ FOR statements are used to set up loops when the number of repetitions of the loop can be specified in advance.

○ The general format is:

FOR *variable* := *initial* TO *final* DO
    statement;

where the *statement* can be single or compound. The *variable* is assigned successive values between *initial* and *final* inclusive, and the *statement* is executed for each value. If *final* is less than *initial*, the *statement* is not executed. *Initial* and *final* can be any expression with an integer or character value.

○ In the general format, TO can be replaced by DOWNTO. Now the *variable* takes successive decreasing values between *initial* and *final*. If *final* is greater than *initial*, the *statement* is not executed.

○ The WRITELN statement causes a carriage return after output, so any subsequent output starts at the beginning of the next line. The WRITE statement does not cause a carriage return, so any subsequent output continues on the current line (if there is room).

```
Ans 7.9   PROGRAM PATTERN (OUTPUT);
          VAR     ROW: INTEGER;
                  CH: CHAR;
          BEGIN
            FOR ROW := 1 TO 4 DO
              BEGIN
                FOR CH := 'Z' DOWNTO 'T' DO
                  WRITE (CH);
                WRITELN ('*');
              END;
          END.
```

Further questions

7.12 Write a program called RAINFALL that will read in 12 real numbers, each representing the rainfall for each month of the year in a particular area. The program should then print out the average monthly rainfall. Use variables called RAIN, TOTAL, and MONTH. Include appropriate text.

7.13 Write a program called PAT4 that will print out the following pattern. Include a procedure called ASTERISKS using a local variable called N. Use a global variable called ROW.

```
*
**
***
****
***
**
*
```

7.14 Write a program called PAT5 that will print out the following pattern. Include a procedure called PRINTLINE using a local variable called L. Use a global variable called P.

```
**********
*
**********
*
**********
*
**********
*
**********
```

Ans 7.10
```
PROGRAM PAT2 (OUTPUT);
VAR      ROW, N: INTEGER;
BEGIN
  FOR ROW := 1 TO 15 DO
    BEGIN
      FOR N := 1 TO 15 DO
        WRITE ('*');
      WRITELN;
    END;
END.
```

Ans 7.11
```
*******
   *
   *
   *
*******
   *
   *
   *
*******
   *
   *
   *
```

Unit 8 Arrays

We can start by thinking of an array as a group of similar variables that share a common name. It is sometimes more convenient to refer to the variables as members of the group than as separate variables.

A good example of using arrays occurs when dealing with a list of data values of the same type, such as the following list of temperature readings:

Temperature
15
8
0
−3
20
1

In a program, we may want to store each temperature value in a different variable. We could do this by declaring six separate variables in the VAR declaration. But an alternative is to declare an array of six variables using just one name, say TEMP, and then identify each variable by means of a special number placed after the array name. This special number is called a *subscript* and it must be enclosed in square brackets. So we could declare an array called TEMP that contains the following six *elements*:

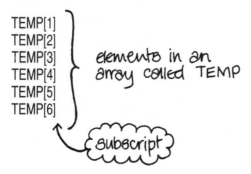

TEMP[1]
TEMP[2]
TEMP[3] elements in an
TEMP[4] array called TEMP
TEMP[5]
TEMP[6]

subscript

An element is a subscripted variable in an array. In the TEMP array, the value of the first element TEMP[1] is 15, the value of the second element TEMP[2] is 8, and so on.

Each array element can be treated like the separate *simple* variables we have used up to now. For example, the statement:

WRITELN (TEMP[4]);

will print out the value of the fourth element (that is −3). Or we can assign a new value (say 14) to the last element by:

TEMP[6] := 14;

Note the difference between an array element called TEMP[6] and a simple variable called TEMP6. TEMP[6] is the sixth element in the array called TEMP, while TEMP6 is a single variable that has no connection with the TEMP array.

As stated earlier, instead of the TEMP array we could have declared six simple variables, called perhaps TEMP1, TEMP2, and so on. At this point there may seem to be little practical difference, but after the next question we will show that arrays can be much more convenient and powerful.

◖ Qu 8.1   For a ten element array called LIST, write statements that will (a) give the value of 67 to the ninth element, (b) print out the value of the last element.

In the examples so far, the subscripts after the array name have been integer numbers. The subscript can also be an integer variable, for example:

U := 5;
WRITELN (TEMP[U]);

which will print out the value of the fifth element of the TEMP array (that is 20). The following statements allow the user to print the value of any particular element in the array:

READ (U);
WRITELN (TEMP[U]);

(The integer variable U would be declared in the normal way in the VAR declaration.)

As noted in Unit 7, FOR statements are frequently used with arrays. For example, the following FOR statement will print the value of each element in the TEMP array:

```
FOR U := 1 TO 6 DO
    WRITELN (TEMP[U]);
```

If six simple variables were used instead of an array, six separate WRITELN statements would be needed to print the temperature values. As the number of elements increases, the greater is the convenience of using arrays compared to simple variables.

◐ Qu 8.2   A program uses an array called PRICE, which contains 50 elements. Write a FOR statement that will print the value of each element on a separate line. Use an integer variable called U.

◐ Qu 8.3   TOTAL is an array of 24 elements. Write a FOR statement that will give each element the value of zero. Use an integer variable called U.

In the above FOR statement examples, we have used a variable called U to identify an element in an array. Where appropriate, we will adopt this practice as a convention. (Often a variable called I is used instead of U; but the letter I can be confused with the digit 1 and is less readable.)

We have seen examples where the subscript is an integer number or variable. However, the subscript can be *any* expression with an integer value (a real value such as TEMP[3.5] would be meaningless). For example:

```
U := 66;
WRITELN (LIST[U + 1]);
```

will print the value of the 67th element of an array called LIST. Here is another example:

```
IF TEMP[U] < TEMP[U + 1]
THEN WRITELN (TEMP[U])
ELSE WRITELN (TEMP[U + 1]);
```

◐   Qu 8.4   Assume values for the TEMP array shown in the list on page 92. What will be printed when the above IF statement is executed, given that U has the value of 5?

Arrays must be declared in the VAR declaration, like simple variables. The general format is:

VAR *name*: ARRAY[*a..b*] OF *type*;

where *name* is the name of the array; *a* and *b* are integer numbers showing the first and last subscripts of the array; and *type* is the type of data the array can hold.

Thus a declaration for the six element TEMP array is:

VAR TEMP: ARRAY[1..6] OF INTEGER;

and the following:

VAR LIST: ARRAY[1..250] OF REAL;

declares an array called LIST that contains 250 elements.

As the general declaration format shows, an array can hold values of only one type. So, for example, an array cannot hold both real and character values.

◐   Qu 8.5   Write a declaration for an array called ALPHA that is to hold the 26 alphabetic characters.

◐   Qu 8.6   Assume a program contains the declaration in Qu 8.5 for ALPHA, and that the array now holds all 26 letters in alphabetical order. Write one statement using the array that will print the string ABDZ on one line of the screen.

Ans 8.1   (a) LIST[9] := 67;   (b) WRITELN (LIST[10]);

Did you remember the square brackets?

Here is a complete program containing an array:

```
PROGRAM NUMBERS (INPUT, OUTPUT);
VAR       U: INTEGER;
          LIST: ARRAY[1..5] OF INTEGER;
BEGIN
  FOR U := 1 TO 5 DO
    READ (LIST[U]);
  FOR U := 5 DOWNTO 1 DO
    WRITELN (LIST[U]);
END.
```

reads values into the array

The first FOR statement in this program reads values into the LIST array. If input is from a terminal, the user would be expected to type in five numbers.

◐   Qu 8.7   Assume the program NUMBERS above is running and the user types in the numbers 3, 6, 9, 12, and 15. (a) What is printed out by the program? (b) What is the value of LIST[4]?

A common requirement is to exchange the values of two elements in an array. For this purpose we will use the parameterized SWAP procedure given on page 67. Assuming this procedure has been declared in a program that processes the array called TEMP, we can write statements such as:

```
SWAP (TEMP[1], TEMP[6]);
```

If the array originally held values shown in the list on page 92, the array will now hold values as follows (writing the list horizontally instead of vertically):

```
1 8 0 −3 20 15
```

Ans 8.2   FOR U := 1 TO 50 DO
               WRITELN (PRICE[U]);

Ans 8.3   FOR U := 1 TO 24 DO
               TOTAL[U] := 0;

The following FOR statement also uses the SWAP procedure:

```
FOR U := 2 TO 6 DO
    IF TEMP[U] > TEMP[1]  ←——————— compares each value
    THEN SWAP (TEMP[U], TEMP[1]);              with the first value
```

◖ **Qu 8.8** Assume this FOR statement is about to be executed and the TEMP array holds values given on page 96. State the order of the values held in the TEMP array after execution of the FOR statement. (An explanation of the answer is given below.)

The FOR statement places the highest value in the first element of the array. After the first execution, the array values are:

8 1 0 −3 20 15

After the second and third executions there is no change. Then after the fourth execution the values are:

20 1 0 −3 8 15

On the final execution there is again no change.

Ans 8.4   1

Ans 8.5   VAR ALPHA: ARRAY[1..26] OF CHAR;

Ans 8.6   WRITELN (ALPHA[1], ALPHA[2], ALPHA[4], ALPHA[26]);

98

Below is a complete program that reads six temperature values, and then prints out the values with the highest value first. The procedure FIND1ST includes the FOR statement discussed above.

```
PROGRAM HIGHTEMP (INPUT, OUTPUT);
VAR        U: INTEGER;
           TEMP: ARRAY[1..6] OF INTEGER;

PROCEDURE SWAP (VAR X, Y: INTEGER);
VAR        STORE: INTEGER;
BEGIN
  STORE   := X;
  X       := Y;
  Y       := STORE;
END;

PROCEDURE FIND1ST;
BEGIN
  FOR U := 2 TO 6 DO
    IF TEMP[U] > TEMP[1]
    THEN SWAP (TEMP[U], TEMP[1]);
END;

BEGIN (* main program *)
  FOR U := 1 TO 6 DO
    READ (TEMP[U]);
  FIND1ST;
  FOR U := 1 TO 6 DO
    WRITELN (TEMP[U]);
END.
```

◑ **Qu 8.9** Modify the program HIGHTEMP above so the second highest temperature will appear in the second position in the printed list (in addition to the highest temperature appearing in the first position). Use another procedure called FIND2ND.

Ans 8.7   (a) 15 12 9 6 3 (printed on separate lines)
           (b) 12

The program HIGHTEMP and Qu 8.9 have introduced ideas used in sorting a series of numbers into numerical order. Sorting is a common activity in computing, and a complete program for sorting is given in Exercise C-2 (page 106). You may like to try writing such a program, or at least think about the approach, before reaching the Exercise. (The program in Exercise C-2 reads real values into a 20 element array called LIST, sorts them into ascending numerical order, and prints out the sorted list. The program uses the parameterized SWAP procedure and another procedure called SORTUP.)

So far in this Unit we have looked at *one-dimensional* arrays, which contain elements with one subscript. Here we briefly introduce *two-dimensional* arrays, which contain elements with two subscripts.

One-dimensional arrays are typically used for processing lists of data values. Two-dimensional arrays are typically used for processing tables of data values, such as:

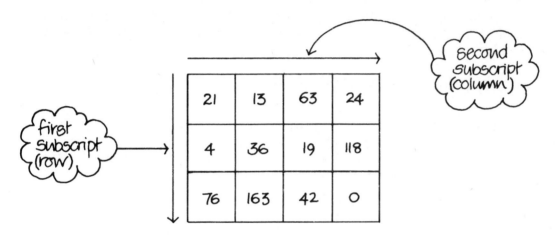

The first subscript of an element identifies a row number, and the second subscript identifies a column number. If the array containing the above data values is called TABLE, then the element in the second row and fourth column (which contains the value 118) is identified by TABLE[2,4]. The following statement will print out the value 163:

        WRITELN (TABLE[3,2]);

Notice the subscripts are separated by commas and are enclosed by a single pair of square brackets.

Ans 8.8   20 1 0 −3 8 15

It is possible to have arrays with three or more dimensions, which contain elements with three or more subscripts. However, apart from Qu 8.10 below, the remaining questions and exercises in this book involve only one-dimensional arrays.

◑   Qu 8.10   Referring to the above table, write a statement that will assign the value held in the box in the top left-hand corner to the box in the bottom right-hand corner. Assume a two-dimensional array called TABLE has been declared.

Finally, we briefly return to the topic of string variables. On page 59 we noted that some versions of Pascal do not provide a STRING type. In the absence of a STRING type, string variables must be set up using character arrays. Take for example the string variable called NAME in the program GREETING on page 58. Assuming names do not exceed 15 characters, we can declare NAME by:

        VAR NAME: PACKED ARRAY[1..15] OF CHAR;

Notice we have specified a *packed* array. Packed arrays take up less space in memory and are normally used for holding character strings.

Having declared the array, characters can be read into and written from the array using techniques that will be demonstrated in Exercise C-1 (page 104).

Ans 8.9   Insert the following procedure declaration before the main program:

```
PROCEDURE FIND2ND;
BEGIN
  FOR U := 3 TO 6 DO
    IF TEMP[U] > TEMP[2] THEN SWAP (TEMP[U], TEMP[2]);
END;
```

Then insert the procedure call FIND2ND after the call FIND1ST in the main program.

Summary (Unit 8)

○ An array is a group of variables of the same type that share a common name. Each individual variable is identified by a subscript placed after the array name.

○ A *subscript* can be any expression with an integer value, and must be enclosed by square brackets.

○ A subscripted variable belonging to an array is called an array *element*. A separate variable not belonging to an array is called a *simple* variable.

○ An array must be declared in the VAR declaration. The general format is:

VAR *name*: ARRAY[*a..b*] OF *type*;

where *name* is the name of the array; *a* and *b* are integer numbers showing the first and last subscripts of the array; and *type* is the type of data the array can hold.

○ One-dimensional arrays contain elements with one subscript, and are typically used for processing lists. Two-dimensional arrays contain elements with two subscripts, and are typically used for processing tables. It is possible to have arrays with three or more dimensions.

Further questions

8.11 Write a program called BACKWARDS that will read a word containing nine letters and then print it out backwards. Use an array called WORD. Allow for leading spaces before the first letter of the word.

8.12 Write a program called QUALITY that will read the points gained in 12 quality control tests into an integer array called RESULT. If two or more of the results are below 90 points, then print out all the results. Otherwise print out the word ACCEPTED. Use a variable called LOWRESULTS to count the number of results below 90.

8.13 The following program will count and print out the number of votes gained by two candidates in an election. The two candidates are identified by the numbers 1 and 2.

```
PROGRAM VOTES (INPUT, OUTPUT);
VAR        CAND, TOTAL1, TOTAL2: INTEGER;
BEGIN
   TOTAL1 := 0;
   TOTAL2 := 0;
   READ (CAND);
   WHILE CAND <> −9 DO
     BEGIN
       IF CAND = 1 THEN TOTAL1 := TOTAL1 + 1;
       IF CAND = 2 THEN TOTAL2 := TOTAL2 + 1;
       READ (CAND);
     END;

   WRITELN ('Candidate 1 ', TOTAL1);
   WRITELN ('Candidate 2 ', TOTAL2);
END.
```

Rewrite the program for 12 candidates. We suggest you use an array, called TOTAL.

Ans 8.10   TABLE[3,4] := TABLE[1,1]

Exercises C

Exercise C-1

Sometimes we do not know the number of values an array needs to hold. In this case, we must declare an array large enough to hold the maximum number of values involved, which means that later elements in the array will sometimes be empty.

The program opposite searches for values in a series that are above the average for that series. We do not know the actual number of values in the series, but assume it does not exceed 15. We now need an end of data marker to show the end of the series, and we need to count the values as they are read in (using the COUNT variable).

The WHILE loop includes a multiple condition: the loop is executed until -9999 is typed or until 15 values have been typed.

(a) If the user types in the numbers: 4, 6, 5, 0, 5, 4, and -9, what is then printed out by the program?

(b) Rewrite the program called NUMBERS on page 96 assuming 30 or less numbers will be typed in. Use -1111 as an end of data marker. Include appropriate text and comments.

```
PROGRAM ABOVEAVERAGE (INPUT, OUTPUT);
(* finds values above average in a series of up to 15 integers *)

VAR  NUM,                        (* value read in *)
     COUNT,                      (* count of values *)
     TOTAL,                      (* total of values *)
     U          : INTEGER;       (* array element *)
     AVERAGE : REAL;             (* average of values *)
     SERIES    : ARRAY[1..15]
                 OF INTEGER;     (* all values in the series *)

BEGIN
  COUNT := 0;
  TOTAL := 0;
  WRITELN ('You can type up to 15 integer numbers. If there are');
  WRITELN ('less, type -9999 after the last number');

  (* read values into the array *)
  READ (NUM);
  WHILE (NUM <> -9999) AND (COUNT <= 15) DO
    BEGIN
      COUNT := COUNT + 1;
      SERIES[COUNT] := NUM;
      TOTAL := TOTAL + NUM; (* total is needed to find average *)
      READ (NUM);
    END;

  (* find average of the series *)
  AVERAGE := TOTAL / COUNT;

  (* print values above average *)
  WRITELN ('The following numbers are above the average:');
  FOR U := 1 TO COUNT DO
    IF SERIES[U] > AVERAGE
    THEN WRITELN (SERIES[U]);
END.
```

Exercise C-2

The program opposite sorts numbers into ascending order. The numbers are read into an array called LIST, then sorted by the SORTUP procedure, and then printed out in order.

The variable POSN represents positions in the final sorted list. The FOR statement in the SORTUP procedure examines each position in turn and places the appropriate value in it. There is no need to examine the last position since if all previous 19 positions have the correct number, the last position must also have the correct number.

The SWAP procedure has been nested in the SORTUP procedure, since SWAP is used only in SORTUP. There is no great advantage in nesting procedures in a short program like this, but it does demonstrate a nested procedure. Also for demonstration purposes, parameters have been used in the SWAP procedure.

When answering the following questions, use the approach and names adopted in the program opposite except where otherwise stated:

(a) Write a program to sort 12 letters into alphabetical order, given A is low and Z is high. Use the parameterized SKIPREAD procedure introduced in Unit 6 to allow for leading spaces before a letter.

(b) Write a program to sort 15 *integer* numbers into *descending* order. Replace the SORTUP procedure by a procedure called SORTDOWN, and use the SWAP procedure without parameters. The program should also print the total of the numbers. Include appropriate text.

Comments   Sorting is a common activity in computing. For example, employee and customer records are usually sorted before being processed and updated.

There are several sorting methods, some more efficient than others in terms of time taken and memory used. The program opposite uses the *exchange* sort method, which is reasonably efficient for small amounts of data. Where thousands of data values are to be sorted, other more efficient (and more complex) methods may be used.

```
PROGRAM SORT (INPUT, OUTPUT);
(* sorts 20 real numbers into ascending order *)

VAR       U: INTEGER;
          LIST: ARRAY[1..20] OF REAL;

PROCEDURE SORTUP;
VAR       POSN: INTEGER;

  PROCEDURE SWAP (VAR X, Y: REAL);
  VAR       STORE: REAL;
  BEGIN
    STORE := X;
    X     := Y;
    Y     := STORE;
  END;

BEGIN (* sortup *)
  FOR POSN := 1 TO 19 DO
    FOR U := POSN + 1 TO 20 DO
      IF LIST[U] < LIST[POSN]
      THEN SWAP (LIST[U], LIST[POSN]);
END;

BEGIN (* main program *)
  FOR U := 1 TO 20 DO
    READ (LIST[U]);
  SORTUP;
  FOR U := 1 TO 20 DO
    WRITELN (LIST[U]);
END.
```

examines each position in turn

Postscript

This book has discussed the following areas:

input and output statements (READ, WRITE, and WRITELN)
assignment statements
repetition statements (REPEAT, WHILE, and FOR)
decision statements (IF-ELSE)
simple variables (real, integer, and character)
procedures
arrays

Several topics have been introduced but not covered in detail: multiple conditions and CASE statements (page 45); parameters in procedures (page 67); functions (page 70); two-dimensional arrays (page 98); and string variables (page 58 and 100). In particular, we would emphasize the importance of parameters in procedures and functions, and note that the two types of parameter (*variable* and *value* parameters) have not been covered.
Below we briefly outline some topics that have been omitted from the book:

READLN statements

READLN statements differ from READ statements in one main respect. After a READLN statement is executed, the remainder of the current line is skipped over and any subsequent input is taken from the beginning of the next line. READLN statement are discussed further in the Appendix (page 114).

Boolean variables

A variable can be declared as type BOOLEAN. Boolean variables are used to hold the results of conditions, and can take two values: TRUE and FALSE. It is never essential to use boolean variables, but they can improve the readability and efficiency of programs.

Enumerated types	Pascal provides four standard types: REAL, INTEGER, CHAR, and BOOLEAN (and sometimes a fifth, STRING). In addition, a user can define his own data types, which are called *enumerated* types. Enumerated types are declared in a TYPE declaration, which precedes the VAR declaration in programs. Like BOOLEAN types, enumerated types can increase the readability and efficiency of programs.
Files	In this book we have assumed all input is from a keyboard and all output is to a video screen. However, input and output can be from and to other media, including magnetic tape and disk where data is held in *files*. A data file holds a series of related data items, which can be read individually by a program. A file must be declared in the VAR declaration. (Data files are not available on some small microcomputers.)
Data structures	A simple variable can hold only a single value, such as a number or a character. A data structure can hold more than one single value. Two examples of data structures we have seen are arrays and files. Other data structures are *records* and *sets*. Records typically hold data similar to that contained in "manual" records (e.g. an employee record may contain name, address, age, salary, etc.); sets are used in mathematical and modelling applications. Records can be linked together to form larger data structures.
GOTO statements	As the name implies, a GOTO statement can be used to jump to another specified statement in a program. For reasons that will be given below, using GOTO statements is not encouraged in Pascal, and they can usually be avoided by using the repetition and decision statements described in this book.

The last topic we consider here is programming strategy. We have not explicitly referred to strategy up to now for two reasons: first, Pascal by its nature tends to encourage good programming strategy; and second, strategy is more difficult to illustrate with shorter programs, which have been used in this book, than with longer programs.

There are two main aspects to good strategy. The first is to use *top-down* design (sometimes known as *stepwise refinement*). Here a task to be performed by a program is broken down into a series of sub-tasks. These in turn may be broken down further, until a number of self-contained units or modules are identified. These units can then become the blocks of the program (see pages 70 and 71). To a large extent, top-down design simply formalizes a basic human technique for solving problems by breaking them down into smaller more manageable units. Most comprehensive books on Pascal contain an example of top-down design.

The second aspect of strategy is to ensure the series of statements within a block are well organized or *structured*. This is helped by a full range of repetition statements (REPEAT, WHILE, and FOR) and a full decision statement (IF-ELSE) (we specify "full" here since some languages do not provide all these statements). Deviations from the sequential execution of statements should be made using only these repetition and decision statements where possible. In particular, structured techniques minimize or avoid using GOTO statements to jump about in programs; frequent or indiscriminate use of GOTO statements can lead to "spaghetti" programs with multiple tangled paths that are very difficult to read, understand, and correct.

A block-structured language with a full range of repetition and decision statements, like Pascal, lends itself to producing well designed and well structured programs. Some languages do not provide blocks or a full range of statements and, as a result, using good strategy can be more difficult (but not impossible).

Programming strategy is a vitally important subject and should be studied further by the serious programmer.

*   *   *   *   *

There are many comprehensive books on Pascal available that cover the topics listed in this Postscript, including:

"Pascal: An Introduction to Methodical Programming", W. Findlay and D. A. Watt, Pitman, Third Edition 1985 (which emphasizes programming strategy).

"Introduction to Pascal", J. Welsh and J. Elder, Prentice-Hall, Second Edition 1982 (which includes a full coverage of more advanced topics).

"Introduction to Pascal—Second Edition", N. Graham, Castle House Publications (UK) and West Publishing Co. (USA) 1983 (which includes UCSD Pascal).

Appendix: Running a Pascal program

This Appendix gives a brief introduction to running Pascal programs on a computer. For further information you will need to consult the reference manual for the computer you are using. Even if you do not have access to a computer, you should still read through this Appendix to get more of an idea of what happens when a program is run.

The last section of the Appendix gives further information on output format, which is of more immediate interest when you have access to a computer and can run a program.

Developing and running a program

Most computers that run Pascal programs must have at least one disk drive attached. The drive contains a magnetic disk (or disks) that holds the Pascal system and, often, the programs you write. With some computers you must first place the disk (or disks) holding the Pascal system into the disk drive and, perhaps, type in special instructions or *commands* on the keyboard. With other computers, the Pascal system may be on a disk that is already available to the computer. (Recent systems may have the Pascal system stored on a silicon chip inside the computer; such systems may not always need a disk drive.)

Before going further we must introduce two new terms, *program file* and *compiler*:

Program file   Programs are held on disk in named areas referred to as *files* (program files are similar to data files introduced on page 109, except a program file now holds a program rather than data). With some systems you must always initially supply a name for the program file, and the program is subsequently identified by that filename. With other systems, the current program is assumed if a filename is not specified.

Compiler   Internally, a computer does not use symbols such as letters or numbers but uses a special code of its own called *machine code*. A computer must translate a program written in Pascal into machine code before it can run the program. With Pascal, the most common method of translation is to use a *compiler*, and the translation process is called *compilation*. A compiler is itself a program and is part of the Pascal system stored on disk (or on a chip).

We can now outline the process of developing and running a Pascal program, which involves three main stages:

1 Typing in Typing in or amending a program is usually called *editing*. You may first need to type a command such as EDIT or E, followed in some systems by a filename (here we will use the filename MYFILE); in other systems a filename is not needed for editing the current program.

2 Compiling When a program has been typed in (or amended), it must be compiled. Examples of commands to compile a program are:

```
        PASCAL, C, MYFILE
or      COMPILE MYFILE.PASCAL
or      C
```

The last command will compile the current program in some systems. The compiler detects any *syntax* errors in the program such as missing semicolons, misspelt statement names, or missing keywords like BEGIN. If there are any errors, messages are displayed on the screen and the compilation is reported as unsuccessful. You must then return to stage 1 and correct the errors.

3 Running If the compilation is successful, the program can be run. Examples of commands are:

```
        PASCAL, R, MYFILE
or      RUN MYFILE.PASCAL
or      R
```

The last command will run the current program in some systems. You may next be asked to specify devices for input and output of data, such as keyboard, screen, disk, tape, and printer (or keyboard and screen may be assumed by default). The program will now run, accepting input and producing output. For example, the program ADDITION on page 4 will output the number 26, and the program EXAMPLE1 on page 28 will accept an integer number as input.

There are several variations to these stages and you must consult the reference manual for your computer for details. For example, stages 2 and 3 can sometimes be combined, so that if the compilation is successful the program will run immediately. Or an extra stage may be needed after compilation to *link* the program to special Pascal system routines.

A program can be run again by carrying out stage 3. But if any amendments are made (even by one letter), the whole program must be re-compiled.

A program can always be *saved* on disk or tape for future use. This is sometimes done automatically with computers that have a disk drive attached.

Finally, we should mention a less commonly used method of translating Pascal programs. This method uses an *interpreter* rather than a compiler. An interpreter translates a program statement by statement as it is run. Thus, unlike a compiled program, an interpreted program is translated *every* time it is run. This means programs take longer to run, which becomes significant with larger programs. But using an interpreter does cut out the separate translation stage, which can be more convenient when there are many amendments or errors.

The RETURN key

All computers have a key marked RETURN or NEWLINE or something similar. In this book we have called it the RETURN key. After the key is pressed, any subsequent input or output is displayed starting at the beginning of the next line. This action is sometimes called a *carriage return* because of the similarity to starting a new line on a typewriter.

The RETURN key often has the additional function of making the input displayed on the current line available to the system. For example, when typing in commands we looked at in the last section such as:

```
        EDIT MYFILE
or      PASCAL, C, MYFILE
or      R
```

you must press the RETURN key before the command is executed.

With some systems, a similar rule applies when a program is running and you are typing in input data. There may be several data items on the current line, but none are made available to the program until you press the RETURN key. This need to press RETURN to enter data has been assumed in this book.

However, with other systems, input data is made available to a program immediately it is typed in with no need to press the RETURN key. This has implications for the layout of output on the screen, which are discussed in the next section.

Output format

As noted above, in this book we have assumed the RETURN key must be pressed to make data available to a program. Since the RETURN key also causes a carriage return, any output following the input data will start on a new line. However, with systems that make data available immediately without pressing RETURN, any subsequent output may continue on the same line, giving a poor layout.

The problem arises mainly with character data. With numeric data, the user normally presses RETURN after the last item on a line (to indicate the end of the item); but he could type a space instead, which could then make the data available to the program without a carriage return.

The problem can be avoided in two ways:

1 Insert a blank WRITELN statement after a READ statement. This causes a carriage return before any subsequent WRITELN or WRITE statements are executed. (For example, in the program PETBILL in page 57, insert a blank WRITELN statement after the statement on line 8).

2 Use a READLN statement instead of a READ statement. A READLN statement causes a carriage return after reading data (page 108).

Incidentally, the READLN statement can also overcome the problem of the space introduced by the action of the RETURN key, which can cause errors when reading character data (see page 56). The READLN statement causes subsequent input to be taken from the beginning of the next input line, thus skipping over the space at the end of the previous line introduced by the RETURN key.

We have not used the READLN statement in this book because it produces different effects on different computers. It can be more convenient than the READ statement for reasons given above, and you should investigate its action on your computer. But if you want to write *portable* programs, that is programs that will run on different computers, it is best to avoid the READLN statement.

Formatting information   In Unit 1 we introduced the topic of formatting information in WRITELN statements (page 9) but stated we would not use it in programs in this book. However, when running programs, formatting information can be important for the readability of output.

Take the statement on page 51:

WRITELN ('KILOGRAMS REMAINING =', KILOS);

where KILOS is an integer variable with a value of 67. With some computers, several spaces may be left before the number 67; with other computers, no spaces will be left. To obtain any particular spacing, we must specify the width in characters of the output *field* for KILOS; if the number of characters to be printed is less than the field width, leading spaces are inserted. The field width is specified by placing a colon and number after KILOS. For example:

WRITELN ('KILOGRAMS REMAINING =', KILOS :3);   *field width*

states the output field width is three characters. Printing the value of KILOS takes up two characters (67), so an extra space is inserted before the 6. Now there will be one space between the equals sign and 67 (as shown on page 51). To insert say ten spaces, we would replace the number 3 in the above statement by the number 12.

Now suppose KILOS is a real variable with a value of 67.5. Without formatting information, this value would be printed using E notation (see page 10). We can avoid the E notation by adding a second colon and number:

WRITELN ('KILOGRAMS REMAINING =', KILOS :5 :1);   *decimal places*

The second colon and number specify that real values are to be printed in normal form, and the second number itself (here 1) specifies the number of decimal places. So the value of KILOS will be printed in normal form to one place of decimals.

The first formatting number still specifies the field width, which is now five characters. Printing the value of KILOS takes up four characters (67.5) so, to insert a space between the equals sign and 67.5, we have specified a field width of 5. To insert ten spaces, we would specify a field width of 14.

Formatting information can be given for any expression in a WRITELN (or a WRITE) statement, for example:

WRITELN (NUM + 2.75 :7 :2);

If NUM has a value of 9, the output of this statement will be 11.75 with two leading spaces.

As a final example, the statement:

WRITELN (NUM :4 :2, NUM * 2 :10 :2);

will produce the following output if NUM has the value 2.06:

2.06   4.12

with six spaces between the two numbers.

Answers to Further Questions and Exercises

Unit 1

1.8   No semicolon after the first WRITELN statement.
No full stop after END.

1.9   PROGRAM COST (OUTPUT);
BEGIN
   WRITELN ((6 * 5.95) + (25 * 0.49));
   WRITELN (5.95 * 0.08);
END.

1.10   PROGRAM EXCHANGE (OUTPUT);
BEGIN
   WRITELN (4 * 2.15);
END.

1.11   PROGRAM COST2 (OUTPUT);
BEGIN
   WRITELN (55 + (55 * 0.10));
   WRITELN (22 + (22 * 0.15));
   WRITELN ((55 * 0.10), (22 * 0.15));
END.

Unit 2

2.12   TAXABLE := PAY − 200;
TAX := TAXABLE * 0.35;
WRITELN (PAY, TAX);

2.13   40 4

2.14   PROGRAM MEAL (OUTPUT);
VAR   PRICE, VAT, SERVICE, TOTAL: REAL;
BEGIN
   PRICE   := 7.5;
   VAT   := PRICE * 0.15;
   SERVICE := PRICE * 0.10;
   TOTAL   := PRICE + VAT + SERVICE;
   WRITELN (PRICE, VAT, SERVICE, TOTAL);
END.

2.15   All integer numbers between zero and 250 inclusive.

Unit 3

3.7   Replace line 4 by:
       READ (PRICE);

3.8   ```
       PROGRAM WEIGHT (INPUT, OUTPUT);
       VAR   KILOS: REAL;
       BEGIN
         READ (KILOS);
         REPEAT
           WRITELN (KILOS * 2.2);
           READ (KILOS);
         UNTIL KILOS = −1;
       END.
       ```

3.9    ```
       PROGRAM TIME (INPUT, OUTPUT);
       VAR       HRS, MINS: INTEGER;
       BEGIN
         READ (HRS, MINS);
         WRITELN ((HRS * 60) + MINS);
       END.
       ```

3.10   ```
       PROGRAM GASBILL (INPUT, OUTPUT);
       VAR   STANDING, RATE, UNIT, CHARGE, TOTAL: REAL;
       BEGIN
         TOTAL := 0;
         READ (STANDING, RATE);
         READ (UNITS);
         REPEAT
           CHARGE := (UNITS * RATE) + STANDING;
           WRITELN (CHARGE);
           TOTAL := TOTAL + CHARGE;
           READ (UNITS);
         UNTIL UNITS = −99;
         WRITELN (TOTAL);
       END.
       ```
       ```

Unit 4

4.10
```
PROGRAM EXAM (INPUT, OUTPUT);
VAR      MARKS1, MARKS2, MARKS3, TOTMARKS: INTEGER;
BEGIN
  READ (MARKS1, MARKS2, MARKS3);
  TOTMARKS:= MARKS1 + MARKS2 + MARKS3;
  IF TOTMARKS >= 45 THEN WRITELN (TOTMARKS);
END.
```

4.11
```
PROGRAM HIGHER (INPUT, OUTPUT);
VAR      C, D: INTEGER;
BEGIN
  READ (C, D);
  IF C > D
  THEN WRITELN (C)
  ELSE WRITELN (D);
END.
```

4.12
```
PROGRAM GASBILL (INPUT, OUTPUT);
VAR      STANDING, RATE, CHARGE, UNITS, TOTAL: REAL;
BEGIN
  TOTAL := 0;
  READ (STANDING, RATE);
  READ (UNITS);
  WHILE UNITS <> -99 DO
    BEGIN
      CHARGE := (UNITS * RATE) + STANDING;
      WRITELN (CHARGE);
      TOTAL := TOTAL + CHARGE;
      READ (UNITS);
    END;
  WRITELN (TOTAL);
END.
```

Unit 5

5.13
```
PROGRAM LICENCE (INPUT, OUTPUT);
VAR      MONTH: INTEGER;
BEGIN
  WRITELN ('TYPE MONTH NUMBER (1 TO 12)');
  READ (MONTH);
  IF MONTH > 9
  THEN WRITELN ('£55')
  ELSE WRITELN ('£35');
END.
```

```
5.14    PROGRAM WINE (INPUT, OUTPUT);
        VAR        BOTTLES: INTEGER;
                   ANSWER : CHAR;
                   CHARGE : REAL;
        BEGIN
          WRITELN ('Type no. of bottles');
          READ (BOTTLES);
          WHILE BOTTLES <> -99 DO
            BEGIN
              WRITELN ('Is delivery required? Y or N');
              REPEAT READ (ANSWER) UNTIL ANSWER <> ' ';
              IF ANSWER = 'Y' THEN CHARGE := BOTTLES * 2.45 + 3
                             ELSE CHARGE := BOTTLES * 2.45;
              WRITELN ('WINE CHARGES ', CHARGE);
              WRITELN ('Type no. of bottles');
              READ (BOTTLES);
            END;
        END.

5.15    PROGRAM AB (INPUT, OUTPUT);
        VAR        CH: CHAR;
                   ACOUNT, BCOUNT: INTEGER;
        BEGIN
          ACOUNT := 0;
          BCOUNT := 0;
          REPEAT
            READ (CH);
            IF CH = 'A' THEN ACOUNT := ACOUNT + 1;
            IF CH = 'B' THEN BCOUNT := BCOUNT + 1;
          UNTIL CH = '.';
          WRITELN ('A =', ACOUNT);
          WRITELN ('B =', BCOUNT);
        END.
```

Unit 6

```
6.8     PROCEDURE READAY;
        BEGIN
          WRITELN ('Type weekday number (Mon =1, Fri = 5)');
          READ (DAY);
          REPEAT
            IF DAY > 5
            THEN WRITELN ('Number exceeds 5. Please re-type);
          UNTIL DAY <= 5;
        END;
```

6.9   PROGRAM TIME (INPUT, OUTPUT);
      VAR   HRS, MINS: INTEGER;

      PROCEDURE PRINTEXCESS;
      VAR   MINUTES: INTEGER;
      BEGIN
        MINUTES := HRS * 60 + MINS;
        IF MINUTES > 150
        THEN WRITELN ('TIME EXCESS')
        ELSE WRITELN ('TIME NORMAL');
      END;

      BEGIN
        READ (HRS);
        WHILE HRS <> −9 DO
          BEGIN
            READ (MINS);
            PRINTEXCESS;
            READ (HRS);
          END;
      END.

6.10 PROGRAM LOWEST (INPUT, OUTPUT);
      (* program to find the lowest of a series of positive numbers typed in by the user *)

      VAR NUM,   (* to contain each number typed in *)
          LOW: REAL; (* to contain the lowest number *)

      BEGIN
        WRITELN ('Type in numbers (type −9 to finish)');
        READ (NUM);
        (* place the first number into LOW *)
        LOW := NUM;
        WHILE NUM <> −9 DO
          BEGIN
            (* place the lowest number so far into LOW *)
            IF NUM < LOW THEN LOW := NUM;
            READ (NUM);
          END;
        (* LOW now contains the lowest number *)
        WRITELN ('Lowest number =', LOW);
      END.

Unit 7

7.12
```
PROGRAM RAINFALL (INPUT, OUTPUT);
VAR       RAIN, TOTAL: REAL;
              MONTH      : INTEGER;
BEGIN
   TOTAL := 0;
   WRITELN ('Type 12 monthly rainfall figures');
   FOR MONTH := 1 TO 12 DO
     BEGIN
       READ (RAIN);
       TOTAL := TOTAL + RAIN;
     END;
   WRITELN ('Average monthly rainfall =', TOTAL / 12);
END.
```

7.13
```
PROGRAM PAT4 (OUTSIDER);
VAR       ROW: INTEGER;

PROCEDURE ASTERISKS;
VAR       N: INTEGER;
BEGIN
   FOR N := 1 TO ROW DO
     WRITE ('*');
   WRITELN;
END;

BEGIN (* main program *)
   FOR ROW := 1 TO 4 DO
     ASTERISKS;
   FOR ROW := 3 DOWNTO 1 DO
     ASTERISKS;
END.
```

```
7.14    PROGRAM PAT5 (OUTPUT);
        VAR     P: INTEGER;

        PROCEDURE PRINTLINE;
        VAR     L: INTEGER;
        BEGIN
          FOR L := 1 TO 10 DO
            WRITE ('*');
          WRITELN;
        END;

        BEGIN (* main program *)
          FOR P := 1 TO 4 DO
            BEGIN
              PRINTLINE;
              WRITELN ('*');
            END;
          PRINTLINE;
        END.
```

Unit 8

```
8.11    PROGRAM BACKWARDS (INPUT, OUTPUT);
        VAR     U: INTEGER;
                WORD: ARRAY [1..9] OF CHAR;
        BEGIN
          REPEAT READ (WORD[1]) UNTIL WORD[1] <> ' ';
          FOR U:= 2 TO 9 DO
            READ (WORD[U]);
          FOR U:= 9 DOWNTO 1 DO
            WRITE (WORD[U]);
        END.
```

8.12
```
PROGRAM QUALITY (INPUT, OUTPUT);
VAR      U, LOWRESULTS: INTEGER;
            RESULT: ARRAY[1..12] OF INTEGER;
BEGIN
  LOWRESULTS := 0;
  FOR U := 1 TO 12 DO
    BEGIN
      READ (RESULT[U]);
      IF RESULT[U] < 90 THEN LOWRESULTS := LOWRESULTS + 1;
    END;

  IF LOWRESULTS >= 2
  THEN FOR U := 1 TO 12 DO
          WRITELN (RESULT[U])
  ELSE WRITELN ('ACCEPTED');
END.
```

8.13
```
PROGRAM VOTES (INPUT, OUTPUT);
VAR      CAND: INTEGER;
            TOTAL: ARRAY[1..12] OF INTEGER;
BEGIN
  FOR CAND := 1 TO 12 DO
    TOTAL[CAND] := 0;

  READ (CAND);
  WHILE CAND <> -9 DO
    BEGIN
      TOTAL[CAND] := TOTAL[CAND] + 1;
      READ (CAND);
    END;

  FOR CAND := 1 TO 12 DO
    WRITELN ('Candidate ', CAND, TOTAL[CAND]);
END.
```

Exercises A

A-1 (a) 11 8 88
     (b) 6 10 60
     (c) nothing is printed out

```
A-2   PROGRAM HOTEL2 (INPUT, OUTPUT);
      VAR      NIGHTS, TOTNIGHTS: INTEGER;
               RATE, CHARGE, TOTCHARGE: REAL;

      BEGIN
        TOTNIGHTS := 0;
        TOTCHARGE := 0;
        READ (NIGHTS);
        WHILE NIGHTS <> -99 DO
          BEGIN
            IF NIGHTS = 1
            THEN RATE := 15
            ELSE IF NIGHTS <= 7
                    THEN RATE := 12
                    ELSE IF NIGHTS <= 28
                            THEN RATE := 10
                            ELSE RATE := 7.5;
            CHARGE := NIGHTS * RATE;
            WRITELN (NIGHTS, RATE, CHARGE);
            TOTNIGHTS := TOTNIGHTS + NIGHTS;
            TOTCHARGE := TOTCHARGE + CHARGE;
            READ (NIGHTS);
          END;
        WRITELN (TOTNIGHTS);
        WRITELN (TOTCHARGE);
      END.

A-3   PROGRAM WAGES (INPUT, OUTPUT);
      VAR      HRS, PAY: REAL;
      BEGIN
        READ (HRS);
        IF HRS <= 40
        THEN PAY := HRS * 2.35
        ELSE IF HRS <= 50
                THEN PAY := (40 * 2.35) + (HRS - 40) * 3.35
                ELSE PAY := (40 * 2.35) + (10 * 3.35) + (HRS - 50) * 4.35;
        WRITELN (HRS, PAY);
      END.
```

Exercises B

B-1 (a) There are only 7 seats available
Please retype number required

(b) 7 seats booked. Thank you
Flight AB24 fully booked

(c) 5 seats booked. Thank you
Flight AB24: 2 seats available
Please type number of seats required

B-2 (a) Total answering Yes: 1552
Total answering No: 1262

Total of males answering Yes: 737
Total over age 40 answering Yes: 1171

(b) Declare NOUN25 as an integer variable

Add to the beginning of the main program:
NOUN25 := 0;

Add to the procedure NOREPLIES:
IF AGE < 25 THEN NOUN25 := NOUN25 + 1;

Add to the end of the main program:
WRITELN ('Total under age 25 answering No: ', NOUN25);

(c) Declare TOTAL as an integer variable

Add to the beginning of the main program:
TOTAL := 0;

Add to the WHILE loop in the main program (before SKIPREAD (REPLY)):
TOTAL := TOTAL + 1;

Add to the end of the main program:
WRITELN ('Total answering the question: ', TOTAL);

Exercises C

C-1 (a) The following numbers are above the average:

6
5
5

(b) PROGRAM NUMBERS (INPUT, OUTPUT);
(* prints up to 30 integers in reverse order *)

```
VAR NUM,                     (* value read in *)
    COUNT,                   (* count of values *)
    U      : INTEGER;        (* array element *)
    LIST   : ARRAY[1..30]
               OF INTEGER;   (* all values read in *)
BEGIN
  COUNT := 0;
  WRITELN ('You can type up to 30 integer numbers. If there');
  WRITELN ('are less, type -1111 after the last number');

  (* read values into the array *)
  READ (NUM);
  WHILE (NUM <> -1111) AND (COUNT <= 30) DO
    BEGIN
      COUNT := COUNT + 1;
      LIST[COUNT]:= NUM;
      READ (NUM);
    END;

  (* print values in reverse order *)
  WRITELN ('Numbers in reverse order are:');
  FOR U:= COUNT DOWNTO 1 DO
    WRITELN (LIST[U]);
END.
```

C-2   (a) PROGRAM SORT (INPUT, OUTPUT);

```
(* sorts 12 letters into alphabetical order *)

VAR       U: INTEGER;
          LIST: ARRAY[1..12] OF CHAR;

PROCEDURE SKIPREAD (VAR CH: CHAR);
BEGIN (* skipread *)
  REPEAT
    READ (CH);
    UNTIL CH <> ' ';
END;

PROCEDURE SORTUP;
VAR       POSN: INTEGER;

  PROCEDURE SWAP (VAR X, Y: CHAR);
  VAR     STORE: CHAR;
  BEGIN (* swap *)
    STORE := X;
    X      := Y;
    Y      := STORE;
  END;

BEGIN (* sortup *)
  FOR POSN := 1 TO 11 DO
    FOR U := POSN +1 TO 12 DO
      IF LIST[U] < LIST[POSN]
      THEN SWAP (LIST[U], LIST[POSN]);
END;

BEGIN (* main program *)
  FOR U := 1 TO 12 DO
    SKIPREAD (LIST[U]);
  SORTUP;
  FOR U := 1 TO 12 DO
    WRITE (LIST[U]);
END.
```

Did you remember to specify CHAR types in the SWAP procedure?

C-2 (b) PROGRAM SORT (INPUT, OUTPUT);
(* sorts 15 integer numbers into descending order and finds the total *)

```
VAR      U, TOTAL: INTEGER;
         LIST: ARRAY[1..15] OF INTEGER;

PROCEDURE SORTDOWN;
VAR      POSN: INTEGER;

  PROCEDURE SWAP;
  VAR     STORE: INTEGER;
  BEGIN (* swap *)
    STORE      := LIST[U];
    LIST[U]      := LIST[POSN];
    LIST[POSN] := STORE;
  END;

BEGIN (* sortdown *)
  FOR POSN := 1 TO 14 DO
    FOR U := POSN + 1 TO 15 DO
      IF LIST[U] > LIST[POSN]
      THEN SWAP;
END;

BEGIN (* main program *)
  TOTAL := 0;
  WRITELN ('Type 15 integer numbers')
  FOR U := TO 15 DO
    READ (LIST[U]);
  SORTDOWN;
  FOR U := 1 TO 15 DO
    BEGIN
      WRITELN (LIST[U]);
      TOTAL := TOTAL + LIST[U];
    END;
  WRITELN ('Total = ', TOTAL);
END.
```

Index